TWO SCREENPLAYS

Jean Cocteau

TWO SCREENPLAYS
The Blood of a Poet
The Testament of Orpheus

Translated from the French by Carol Martin-Sperry

Marion Boyars · London · New York

Reissued in 1985 by
Marion Boyars Publishers
24 Lacy Road, London SW15 1NL
237 East 39th Street, New York, N.Y. 10016

Reprinted in 1989, 1993

Distributed in Australia and New Zealand by
Peribo Pty Ltd, Terrey Hills, NSW

Photos for *The Blood of a Poet* by Sacha Masour, Paris.
Photos for *The Testament of Orpheus* by Lucien Clergue, Arles.

British Library Cataloguing in Publication Data
Cocteau, Jean
    Two screen plays.
    1. Moving-picture plays   2. Moving-pictures,
    French
    I. Title
    791.43'72   PN1997

Library of Congress Cataloging in Publication Data
Cocteau, Jean, 1889–1963.
    Two screenplays.
    Translation of: Le sang d'un poète and Le testament d'Orphée.
    Previously published: New York: Orion Press, 1968.
    Bibliography: p
    1. Cocteau, Jean, 1889–1963 — Translations, English.
    2. Moving-picture plays.   I. Cocteau, Jean, 1889–1963.
    Testament d'Orphée. English. 1985.   II. Title.   III. Title:
    Blood of a poet.   IV. Title: Testament of Orpheus.
PQ2605.015A25   1985   842'.912   84–14589

ISBN 0 7145 0580 3 (paperback)

Printed and bound in Great Britain at
Itchen Printers Ltd, Southampton

CONTENTS

Marion Boyars are also the publishers of
The Art of Cinema by Jean Cocteau.

The Blood of a Poet

Preface (1946)

> *"Most of Aesop's fables have many different*
> *levels and meanings. There are those who make*
> *myths of them by choosing some feature that fits*
> *in well with the fable. But for most of the*
> *fables this is only the first and most super-*
> *ficial aspect. There are others that are more*
> *vital, more essential and profound, that they*
> *have not been able to reach."*
>
> *Montaigne*

It is often said that *The Blood of a Poet* is a surrealist film. However, surrealism did not exist when I first thought of it. On the contrary, the interest that it still arouses probably comes from its isolation from the works with which it is classified. I am speaking of the works of a minority that has opposed and unobtrusively governed the majority throughout the centuries. This minority has its antagonistic aspects. At the time of *The Blood of a Poet,* I was the only one of this minority to avoid the deliberate manifestations of the unconscious in favor of a kind of half-sleep through which I wandered as though in a labyrinth.

I applied myself only to the relief and to the details of the images that came forth from the great darkness of the human body. I adopted them then and there as the documentary scenes of another kingdom.

That is why this film, which has only one style, that, for example, of the bearing or the gestures of a man, presents many surfaces for its exegesis. Its exegeses were innumerable. If I were questioned about any one of them, I would have trouble in answering.

My relationship with the work was like that of a cabinet-maker who puts together the pieces of a table whom the spiritualists, who make the table move, consult.

The Blood of a Poet draws nothing from either dreams or symbols. As far as the former are concerned, it initiates their mechanism, and by letting the mind relax, as in sleep, it lets memories entwine, move and express themselves freely. As for the latter, it rejects them, and substitutes acts, or allegories of these acts, that the spectator can make symbols of if he wishes.

The innumerable faults of *The Blood of a Poet* end up by giving it a certain appeal.

For example, I am most attached to the images. These give it an almost sickening slowness. When I complained of this recently to Gide, he replied that I was wrong, that this slowness was a rhythm of my own, inherent in me at the time I made the film, and that changing the rhythm would spoil the film.

He is undoubtedly right. I am without doubt no longer sensitive to the "element of God" that he speaks of, and that this film uses and abuses. As I know it far too well, I can only observe the acts, and the slowness with which they follow each other hides the rest from me.

Several young people declare that they prefer the dullest reality to such fantasies. Others condemn the film for sacrileges that did not even skim the surface of my mind. Others find wonders in it that I myself would have liked to have put there. Others accuse it of eccentricity. The only valid opinion is that of the technicians. They all agree that the images are lasting and fresh.

No film music is more beautiful or original than Georges Auric's. No photography is more stunning than Périnal's. I was lucky to have such assistance in an enterprise that was so hazardous to begin with.

Above all, what really marks *The Blood of a Poet* is, I think, a complete indifference to what the world finds "poetic," the care taken, on the contrary, to create a vehicle for poetry — whether it is used as such or not.

Is the choice of protagonists not significant? They are amateurs, presences untrained as actors, whose sole duty was to play their role. The statue was Lee Miller, a friend of Man Ray. She had never been in a film before and has never been in a film since. We saw her again in uniform in 1945. The poet was Enrico Rivero, a young Chilean who was chosen for his dispassionate appearance. The Louis XV friend was Jean Desbordes. The black angel was Féral Benga, a jazz dancer. The students were assistant stagehands. Barbette, Pauline Carton, and Odette Thalazac did no more than appear briefly.

In the first version of the film the Viscount and Viscountess of Noailles, the Prince and Princess of Faucigny-Lucinge, and Lady Abdy were in the loge on the left. But when their families saw that they were applauding a suicide, they forbade it. We had to re-shoot the scene of the loges with extras and the friendly presence of Barbette.

Bunuel's *The Golden Age* and *The Blood of a Poet* were both commissioned by the Viscount of Noailles. The religious scandal of one overflowed on to the other. Unobservant people made an intrigue out of it. The two films remained locked up in a safe and the Viscount of Noailles, in return for a gesture unique in France, became the victim of the worst persecutions.

It wasn't until 1931 that we were able to show our films. At the Vieux Colombier, mine, badly printed, badly spliced and badly projected, provoked scandals and battles without even being able to defend itself by its lustre. It was recognized much later, thanks to the universities that asked for it, showed it and considered it a subject for study.

Most of the people who assisted me have become important personalities in the film world. When I meet them we always talk with affection of our shared memories.

I would like to add that chance sent me Georges Périnal,

without whose skill *The Blood of a Poet* would have quickly faded from sight. What a happy and free time it was! I had sent seven telegrams to seven cameramen. Périnal was the first one to show up.

Michel Arnaud was my assistant, as were Page, Viguier and Pomme-Pernette, who is now Marc Allégret's first assistant.

Miss Miller has become a well-known journalist and photographer. Rivero is dead. Desbordes is dead, tortured and killed by the Militia in the rue de la Pompe, 1943.

It is difficult for me, you will admit, to consider such a film without being moved by the circumstances that enriched it. It would be like seeing only the edge of it — unless so much dreaming has given it a halo and the camera has caught in advance those qualities that man can never discover in people and objects.

I have often noticed this phenomenon. It is important for directors to take it into account. They must be careful; they must always be concerned with the choice of their team, good relations and the atmosphere that surrounds the filming.

I know many films that put me to shame. I do not know of one that is less slave to the methods of an art "that is the same age as I" and that therefore never forced me to burden myself with examples.

To sum up, *The Blood of a Poet* and my new film, *Beauty and the Beast* are aimed at the aficionados. It is true that I do not kill the bull according to the rules. But this contempt for the rules is accompanied by a contempt for the danger that excites a large number of people.

J.C.

Credits

THE BLOOD OF A POET *by* Jean Cocteau.

Music by Georges Auric.

With Lee Miller, Pauline Carton, Odette Thalazac, Enrico Rivero, Jean Desbordes, Fernand Dichamps, Lucien Jager, Féral Benga *and* Barbette.

Settings, montage and commentary by Jean Cocteau.

Technical Director:	Michel J. Arnaud
Cameraman:	Georges Périnal
Sound:	Henri Labrély

Sound effects by R.C.A. photophone

Assistant:	Louis Page
Second Cameraman:	Prében Engberg
Set construction:	Y.G. d'Eaubonne
Stills:	Sacha Masour

Flament Orchestra, conducted by Edouard Flament.

Accessories from Maison Berthelin.

Plaster casts by Plastikos.

Text projected on the screen:

Every poem is a coat of arms. It must be deciphered.

How much blood, how many tears in exchange for those axes, those muzzles, those unicorns, those torches, those towers, those martlets, seedlings of stars and those fields of blue.

Free to choose the faces, the shapes, the movements, the tones, the acts, the places that please him, he composes with them a realistic documentary of unreal events. The musician underlines the noises and the silences.

The author dedicates this collection of allegories to the memory of Pisanello, Paolo Uccello, Piero della Francesca, Andrea del Castagno, who were all painters of coats of arms and enigmas.

THE BLOOD OF A POET

The author, masked except for his eyes, holding a plaster hand in his hand, this real hand and the wrist of the other covered by draped cloth, announces that the film is beginning, against a background of studio lamps.

Between the credits, the text, the dedication and the prologue, there is a close-up of the knob of a door that someone is trying to open.

A huge factory chimney. It leans over. It begins to crumble.

The author's voice: *"While the cannons of Fontenoy thundered in the distance, a young man in a modest room ..."*

We hear the cannon. We see a young man drawing at an easel. The paper is transparent, and the eye can follow the line. The young man is naked to the waist, wearing trousers that are rolled up to his calves, cyclist's shoes, white knitted gloves and a Louis XV wig.

The camera moves back and shows the young man (the poet) in profile, in front of the window, finishing the drawing of a face half turned away.

Close-up of a large star-shaped scar on the poet's left shoulder-blade.

The author's voice: *"First episode: the wounded hand, or the scars of the poet."*

The camera shows, in the corner, near the easel, a figure made of pipe-cleaners, whose white frame revolves on the end of a thread.

Close-up of the poet drawing. We hear a knock on the door. He turns around. He looks at his drawing, and there is an expression of shock on his face.

Close-up of the drawing. The mouth is alive. It partially opens, showing solid teeth. The knocking on the door becomes louder and louder.

The camera shows the poet remove the glove from his right hand and rub the drawing, wiping it out as hard as he can. He disappears from the screen to the right.

The poet walks towards the door. He opens it. A friend in a Louis XV costume appears. The poet offers him his hand. His friend, who was about to put out his hand, draws it back. He stares with amazement at the outstretched hand. He rushes away as though blown by the wind and disappears. The door slams.

The staircase. The friend tumbles down it backwards in modern dress.

The poet, alone in the room, looks at the door, smiles, shrugs his shoulders, takes off his wig, throws it onto a hat-rack, and walks towards a washstand.

Above the iron basin and soap dish, a head, like the pipe-cleaner figure, revolves. This white frame turns on the end of a thread, and as it turns it reveals and superimposes its forms.

Close-up of the basin. The poet plunges his hand into it. Bubbles and the sound of bubbles. We notice in the basin

that these bubbles are coming out of a mouth that is in the palm of his right hand, like a wound and the lips of a wound.

View of the poet, from the waist up. He takes his hand out of the basin and looks at it . . .

Close-up of his palm, where the mouth is engraved.

He goes to the window to get a better look at it.

Text: *Taken out of a picture where the naked hand had contracted it like leprosy, the drowned mouth seemed to fade in a little area of white light.*

The actor's hand is substituted by the author's plaster hand.
On it the mouth is partially open and water is flowing out of
it. The mouth is surrounded, as if by a bruise, by a little area
of white light.

The corner of the room, to the right of the window. The poet,
leaning against the wall, is looking at his hand with disgust.
He should have the expression on his face of a man who has
just discovered a leper's sore. He shakes his arm and his hand,
trying to get rid of this phenomenon. The mouth remains
there. It speaks, saying, "Air!" The poet brings his hand to
his ear. The mouth murmurs, "Air!" The actor's hand and

the nape of his neck are substituted by the plaster nape and hand of the author. We see the actor's hand. The mouth, drawn in black on it, opens its lips and says again, "Air!"

The poet (full view) walks towards the window. He breaks a pane with his heel. He puts his arm through and gives the mouth air. He pulls back his arm and looks at his hand. He then looks surreptitiously to his left. He rushes to the door and locks it with his free hand.

He returns to the window, closes his eyes, lifts the mouth to his mouth and glues it there.

He staggers round, a little drunk, with his hand on his face, and falls into an armchair near a round table covered with a soiled cloth. Old newspapers. Oil lamp. Green lampshade.

Close-up of the poet's trembling hand moving towards his neck. The camera follows the hand. It strokes his left shoulder and slides down towards his left breast. Its wet traces can be followed. It goes down, off the screen.

Close-up of his face, turned backwards, from behind the armchair. His hair is hanging down his back. His eyes, enlarged, are painted on his eyelids.

Fade into a mask, white on one side, black on the other, re-volving mechanically on the end of a stick.

The author's voice: *"The next morning...."*

Distant shot of the table, from top to bottom, in the light of the dawn, where the poet has fallen asleep with his profile resting on one arm, and his hand open. Sounds: swallows, a train hurtling past, cocks crowing.

Text (in the author's handwriting) : *The surprises of photography, or how I was caught in a trap by my own film.*
(The author's signature)

Close-up of the sleeping poet, who has become the author in plaster, lying on a plaster arm, with an open plaster hand. The mouth is dreaming inside the hand. It snores gently, whispering disconnected words.

The poet wakes up. Taken from the other side, the picture shows the poet, from behind; a little further away, between the window and the washstand, is a plaster life-size statue of a woman without arms, draped in plaster. The poet stands up. He holds the elbow of his right arm with his left hand.

He walks carefully towards the statue as though it were asleep and he were afraid of waking it.

The statue. The poet walks around it and, with a sudden movement, like an assassin gagging his victim, he puts his right hand over its mouth.

The author's voice: *"It has already proved dangerous to rub against the furniture. Is it not crazy to wake up statues so suddenly from the sleep of centuries?"*

Close-up of his arm. The veins stand out, drawn like the branches of a tree, from the effort he is making.

Close-up of his hand and the statue's face. The statue opens its eyes, or, in other words, eyes appear on the globe of its eyelids. The hand withdraws. The statue moves. Its mouth is alive.

The camera turns to the poet who is looking at his hand, which is now clean, rid of its wound. He wipes it. He sneers at the statue and walks away.

The author's voice: *"Second episode: Do the walls have ears?"*

The statue speaks: *"Do you think it's that simple to get rid of a wound, to close the mouth of a wound?"*

While the statue is speaking, the camera scans the whole room from above. Only the walls remain with neither windows nor door. The poet gropes along the walls, feeling them, and reaches a tall mirror that stands in the place where the door had been. He turns back and . . .

. . . in close-up, shouts at the statue (with the author's voice) : *"Open it for me."*

Close-up of the statue's ironic face. It speaks: *"There is only one way left. You must go into the mirror and walk through."*

Close-up of the poet. He speaks: *"One can't go into mirrors."*

Close-up of the statue: *"I congratulate you. You wrote that one could go into mirrors and you didn't believe it."*

Close-up of the poet. He makes an angry gesture. *"I . . ."*

Close-up of the statue. It interrupts him: *"Try, always try . . ."*

The poet stands in front of the mirror. A chair materializes next to the frame. The poet is startled.

The poet nervously touches the chair. He walks around it. He stands on it. He touches the mirror. His ring strikes it three times, but the sound is heard later than the contact.

The poet hesitates, looks to his left, puts one foot on the edge of the frame, then the other. He grabs hold of the frame with both hands.

View of the poet from the waist up and of his reflection in the mirror.

He looks harder at the mirror than he does at his own reflection. The statue's voice: *"Try . . ."*

Full view of the mirror. The poet throws himself into the glass. His disappearance is accompanied by the sound of a crowd at a firecracker display.

(The mirror has been substituted by a tank of water, the setting is upside-down, the chair nailed on the left. This is all shot from above. The actor plunges. A quick cut back to the room as it was ends the illusion.)

The inside of the mirror. Night. In the distance, the poet, immobile, moves forward on an invisible conveyor that moves him slightly to the left and to the right. With his arms raised and his face lit from below, he comes right up to the camera until he fills the lens.   .

The corridor of a disreputable-looking hotel, with dirty wallpaper and linoleum flooring. There are shoes outside the doors. There is a wall at the end of the corridor that turns to the left.

The author's voice (over the last scene and this scene) : *"The inside of the mirror led to the Hotel des Folies-Dramatiques."*

An Annamese in European dress turns the corner at the end of the corridor. He is reading a newspaper. He stops in front of the third door and speaks through it in Chinese. Then he walks on, still reading. He vanishes before he is out of the camera's range. The poet enters, with his back to the camera. He walks in a strange way, as though he were weighed down and off balance. He is about to pass the first door on the left. He listens, stops, kneels down. He puts his eye to the key-hole.

Close-up of the poet (his face and hands) putting his eye to the key-hole.

The author's voice: *"In the small hours of the night, Mexico,*

the trenches of Vincennes, the boulevard Arago and a hotel room are all the same."

This is what the poet sees and hears indistinctly. The ticking of an alarm clock. A fireplace that is a rock. On this rock that looks like a fireplace is a small statue of the Virgin. In front of this rock-fireplace, stands a Mexican (who looks like the poet). On the left foreground, rifle barrels aimed at him. There is a round of shots. The statue of the Virgin shatters into pieces. The Mexican falls. (This is all in slow motion.) Just after he has fallen, he stands up again in the same position as before and the statue of the Virgin becomes whole again.

Close-up. The poet is watching very closely and shades his eyes with his hands to see better. Another round of shots.

The room. The Mexican has fallen. He stands up again.

The corridor. The poet leaves the key-hole. We hear another round. This camera shot and the following ones are taken from above, and the room is on its side. When the picture shows the room the right way up again, it is this that makes the following action seem so strange: The play of muscles of a back covered with sweat and the paint of the set on which the poet crawls, rubs and rolls. Added to this, the cruel light of a room of crime, a criminal anthropometry department, a prison courtyard.

The poet, struggling against some unknown force, some incomprehensible mistral, moves painfully to the right. He reaches the second door. There is a placard on it that says: FLYING LESSONS.

Close-up of the poet kneeling on the Greek-bordered linoleum, next to a pair of small ballet shoes. The tinkling of bells is heard. He puts his eye to the key-hole — this is what he discovers:

An empty room with straw on the floor. A fireplace. A ladder. A little girl in circus tights with a harness of bells is crouching by the fireplace, while an old governess in a black dress threatens her with a whip. The little girl protects her face with her elbow and stands up. The bells tinkle. The old woman lifts her under her arms and sets her down on top of the fireplace. The bells tinkle. The tip of the whip lashes her. (In the style of the Dickens of "Oliver Twist.")

Close-up of the poet. He moves so as to get the best view possible.

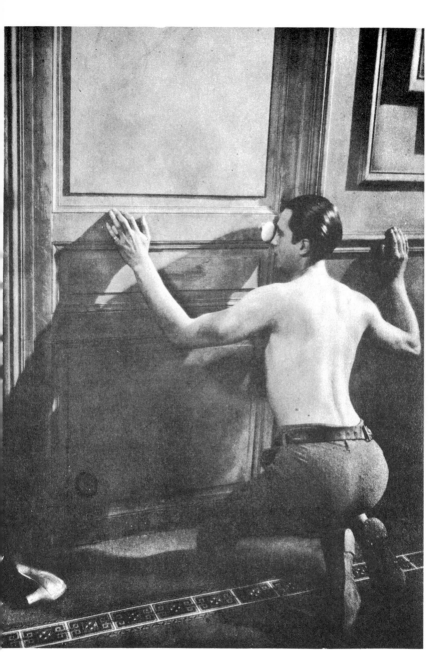

The room. The old woman is standing by the fireplace. The little girl, in the air above the fireplace, seems to be flying in the air, motionless, a kind of constellation of bells. The old woman signals her to keep on flying. The little girl pulls herself up into the emptiness. The camera shows her on the ceiling crawling towards the other corner of the room. The bells tinkle. She passes the wire of the hanging electric light.

The old woman's feet, with buttoned boots. She lifts up her skirts, is agitated and walks over to a ladder that is leaning against the right-hand wall. The camera moves back. The old woman climbs up the ladder and shakes her fist at her pupil.

Close-up of the little girl, who is still on the ceiling, making faces and sticking out her tongue.

The corridor. The poet moves away from the door, tries to keep his balance, props himself up against the wall and makes a great effort to reach the third door. He succeeds.

The author's voice: *"The mysteries of China."*

There are no shoes in front of this door. But the key-hole is blocked with paper. The poet pulls it out, tears it up and throws it away. He looks.

Author's voice: *"Room 19. Celestial Ceiling."*

A ceiling. The electric ceiling light is switched off. The ceiling is lit by an opium lamp that casts Chinese shadows of a pipe and the hand of a smoker. This shadow of the hand pushes a shadow of a needle into the shadow of the pipe. Sound of the opium spluttering. Shadow of the smoke.

Full shot of the corridor. The poet stands up from the key-hole and tries to get a better view. He puts his foot on the door knob, awkwardly raises himself up to the crack above the top of the door and tries to look in and listen. Chinese voices. His foot slips on the door knob. He falls softly, gets up, puts his eye to the key-hole, but . . .

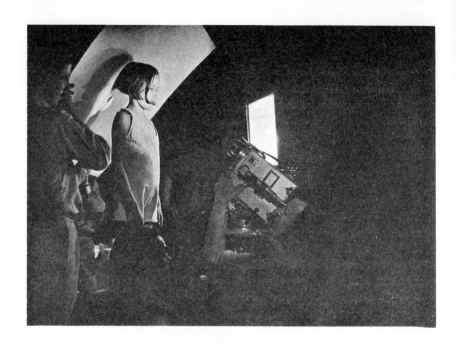

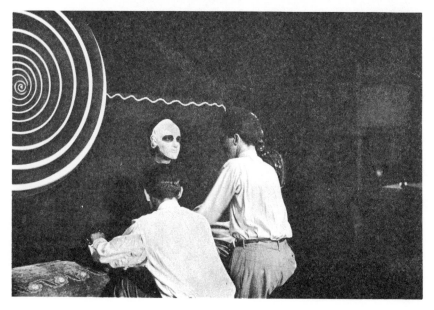

Key-holed shaped close-up of a slit eye approaching from the opposite direction.

The poet drags himself to the next door (do not forget that the set is on its side), which is the last one before the corner of the wall. At the foot of the door on the linoleum are one woman's shoe and one man's shoe.

The author's voice: *"The desperate meetings of the Hermaphrodite took place in room 19."*

His eye at the key-hole, this is what the poet sees: A huge sofa, on the left of which an unending spiral revolves. The sofa is

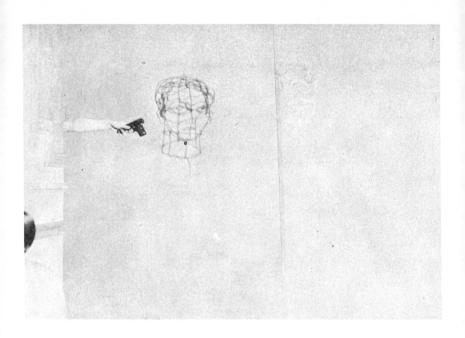

intersected lengthwise by an enormous blackboard. A head, masked in white, appears on it. (Roll of drums.) A chalk drawing appears — torso of an outstretched woman. (Roll of drums.) A real male leg and a real male arm, up to the shoulder, appear.

Close-up of the poet putting his hands against the door and leaning against it. His back arches. The image should be sensual.

The key-hole. The blackboard is covered with stars. (Roll of drums.) More limbs and another torso appear. The Hermaphrodite's hand lifts up a loin cloth and uncovers a sign that says *Danger of death*.

Close-up of the poet's eyes.

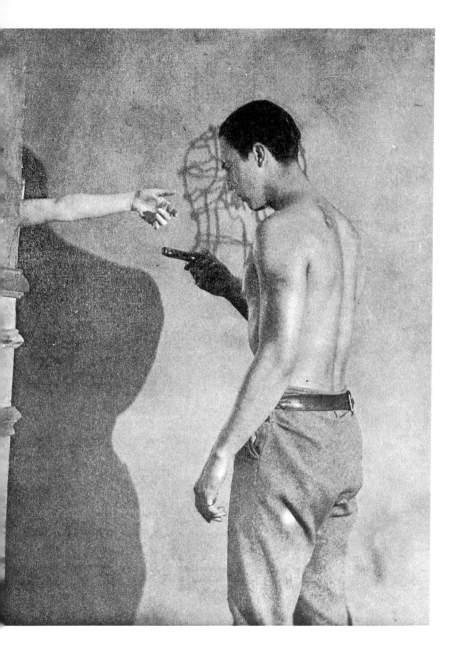

Third key-hole. A mask with real flashing eyes appears. (Drums.) A long Louis XIV wig appears on the mask. (Drums.) A strong leg and arm appear on the female torso. (Drums.) A confused jumble of shirts, petticoats, white ties and socks appear, to the beating of drums, thrown about haphazardly. Man's voice: *"Turn the light off."* Woman's voice: *"No."* Man's voice: *"Yes."* Woman's voice: *"No, leave it."* Sound of water.

The poet stands up and turns to his right.

A woman's arm appears from behind the corner of the wall. The hand of the arm is holding a revolver.

A salesgirl's voice says: *"Directions for use."*

The poet takes hold of the revolver, examines it, and flattens himself against corridor, back to the wall. The shadow of the pipe-cleaner head that was seen in his room revolves on his left. He carries out the instructions given to him by the salesgirl's voice.

The salesgirl's voice: *"Hold the butt of the revolver firmly in your hand. Release the safety catch. Place your index finger on the trigger. Put the barrel against your temple. Shoot."*

View of the poet from the waist up, harshly lit by arc lamps. Sound of the revolver which he puts against his temple. He drops the weapon. The blood spurts out of his temple, flows onto his body and turns into a red cloth that is draped around him. A laurel wreath appears on his head.

The author's voice: *"Glory forever!"*

The poet's closed eyes open. His face expresses anger. He tears off the robe and the crown. He mutters through clenched teeth — *"Merde! Merde! I've had enough ... enough ..."*

Long shot of the corridor. The camera tracks the fleeing poet. He seems to be running against a cross-current. When the set straightens up again, this race along the floor should create a feeling of uneasiness. His flight is accompanied by the double sound of a fast-beating heart and heavy breathing. The poet stops in an impossible position. The heart-beat and the breathing increase three times. His flight continues.

Fade-in on the darkness of night in the mirror. The poet, represented by the white pipe-cleaner figure, walks away. Sound of an approaching tractor.

Fade-in on the opposite side. The pipe-cleaner figure comes closer and closer to the lens until it fills the whole frame. Sound of the tractor going away.

The author's voice: *"Mirrors should reflect a bit more before sending back images."*

The mirror in the room. It expels the poet. Religious choir of childish voices.

Front view of the poet from the waist up. The choir stops singing. The poet clenches his fists and goes toward the statue.

The statue's living head watches him.

The poet takes hold of a hammer and hits the statue. It breaks, and its head splits in two. He keeps on hitting. A cloud of plaster dust rises from the rubble.

Still photo (photography substituted for cinema) of the poet holding the hammer, covered in plaster from head to foot. The author's voice: *"By breaking statues . . ."*

Close-up of the poet's head, like a flour-covered character in an Italian comedy.

The author's voice: *"... one risks ..."*

Shot of buildings in ruins, in the middle of which a white statue is sitting on a pedestal.

The author's voice: *"... turning into one ..."*

Close-up of the statue. It is the poet's.

The author's voice: *"... oneself."*

The camera moves back. The pedestal and the statue are in the Cité Monthiers, where the author played during his childhood after school at Condorcet. It is snowing as in the first chapter of *Les Enfants Terribles.* The Cité has the imprecision of childhood memories; it is larger, more deserted. The poet's statue, covered by a layer of snow, is on the left of a building that is now opposite the Théâtre de l'Oeuvre.

The author's voice: *"Glory, forever Glory! Third episode: The snowball fight."*

A group of schoolboys are jostling and pushing each other through the entrance of the arch that opens onto the rue d'Amsterdam. They are wearing short pants, Basque berets and long, dark woolen cloaks. Their moleskin satchels full of books weigh them down, deform them, giving them an almost crippled air.

It is evening. A gas lamp lights up the muddy snow.

Groups of boys chase each other.

One student is tripped up by another and falls over backwards. (Quick cut.)

Long shot. The students drop their satchels. They pick up the snow and fight each other around the statue.

(Quick cut). One student, under an avalanche of snowballs, facing the wall near the lamp-post begs for mercy with his right hand.

Long shot. The students bombard the statue and destroy it. One of them jumps up onto the pedestal and grabs the head.

Author's voice: *"The warriors."*

The camera near the lamp-post, shows the curved iron-covered steps of the first small private house on the left. At the foot of the steps two students are propping up a friend. He is biting his lips and snapping his fingers. He is limping. The group come closer to the camera, which focuses on his leg and bleeding knee which is bandaged with a handkerchief.

Long shot. The students are using the statue, which has been destroyed, as though it were made of snow, as ammunition for their battle. There is hardly any of it left on the pedestal.

The author's voice: *"The big ones."*

The entrance to the rue d'Amsterdam. Two students arrive, a little older than the others (thirteen and fourteen years old). They are dressed in the same way (bare legs, cloaks, humped by the satchels). They awkwardly light up two cigarettes which they smoke with pursed lips. They sit down in the snow on the lower steps of the curved staircase. They are bombarded. The elder one of them stands up and throws a look of hatred at the camera.

Long shot. The battle is in full swing.

The student with the look of hate slips behind the empty pedestal, leans against it and watches the battlefield.

The camera turns to a young student sitting against the grating of a basement window. Two others, one on each side of him, are pulling the ends of a scarf that is strangling him. He struggles and tries to shout. A few spectators are crouching round making horrible faces at him.

Close-up of the student leaning against the pedestal who seems to be inspecting his troops.

The author's voice: *"Dargelos, the student, was the leader of the pack."*

The camera turns without transition to Dargelos sitting on the steps of the curved staircase, surrounded by his men. He has dropped his satchel. He is making a snowball.

The author's voice: *"A snowball in his hands could become as evil as the knives of Spain."*

Close-up of his friend, alone in the middle of the Cité. He is watching in amazement, his mouth half-open . . .

Dargelos, who tosses back his hair, throws off his hat and cloak and aims furiously at him. He throws the snowball.

It hits the lens of the camera. Another snowball hits the friend in the chest. Shot of him from the waist up being hit, swaying and falling out of view.

Shot of him lying on the ground next to his open satchel, and the books scattered in the snow. The top of the picture reveals several pairs of legs that come up behind the inert body, stop, and then run off. One pair of legs stays there, and unhurriedly walks away.

The camera moves up the pair of legs — it is Dargelos. He walks to the entrance of the street, stops and picks up his satchel.

Close-up of his face. He looks in the direction of the body, sticking out his tongue like a child concentrating in class, shakes back the lock of hair on his forehead and runs off, disappearing through the entrance of the street.

The whole Cité under the snow. It is empty. The body in a little black heap can be seen in the center, facing the pedestal.

The author's voice recites over the picture and the music:
"That blow of marble was a snowball,
And it shattered his heart,
And it shattered the conqueror's tunic,
Shattered the black conqueror whom nothing protects.

*"He stood there, stunned
In the watch-tower of loneliness,
Naked legs under the mistletoe, the golden berries, the holly,
Shattered like a classroom blackboard.*

*"This is often how these blows
Leave school, making blood flow,
These hard snowball blows
That a fleeting beauty gives to the heart."*

"Fourth episode: the Profanation of the Host."

Close-up of the student's head on the snow. Blood is flowing out of his mouth, forming bubbles. He moans, and half-opens his eyes. This picture should be painful to see.

Close-up of the head of Dargelos who seems to be bearing down on the camera.

Back to the suffering head which again closes its eyes. Blood is still escaping from its mouth.

The author's voice: *"That very evening the city was most elegant."*

The camera draws back. Long shot. A lamp and a card table appear on the snow between the pedestal and the body. A woman in an evening gown, who is identical to the statue, is sitting on the left of the table. Opposite her, on the right, is the poet wearing evening clothes. They are holding cards. The Louis XV friend is leaning against the pedestal in the pose of *l'Indifférent,* wearing a black silk mask.

A theatre intermission bell is heard. The camera swings round to the Cité in the background. The windows, with balconies, above the arch, turn into two theatre loges.

The camera tracks in on the loges. A young woman and two old women in low-cut dresses enter the one on the left and sit down near the front. They are escorted by three men who stand behind them.

The camera moves across to the loge on the right. A large woman comes in wearing a low-cut velvet dress. She is escorted

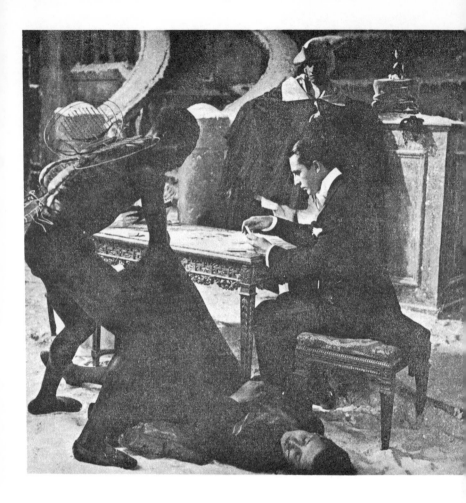

by three men in evening clothes, one with a black patch over his eyes. The large woman sits down and brushes off the snow on the edge of the loge with an ostrich-feather fan. The occupants of the loges observe each other. The spectators on the left seem to be scorning the large woman, who takes revenge by making fun of them, behind her fan, with her escorts. She closes the fan, raises her eyes to the sky and shrugs her shoulders. The intermission bell stops ringing.

The card table — The woman puts down her cards, opens a gold compact, looks at herself in it, closes it and puts it down on the table. Instead of picking up the cards, she picks up her shimmering fan, opens it like a hand of cards, studies it and waves it, turning her head nonchalantly from left to right with no expression whatsoever on her face.

Shot of the Louis XV friend from the waist up. He takes off his mask and puts it down on the pedestal.

The dead child at the foot of the table. Behind him, the legs of the poet in evening clothes.

The author's voice: *"Documentary. Interminable, that's how the cheat imagines his gesture, faster than lightning."*

In slow-motion, the poet's hand, from the top of the picture, slips into the child's jacket, brings out the ace of hearts with his fingers, and disappears out of the top of the frame.

The author's voice: *"The child's guardian angel appeared. He came out of an empty house. He was black in color and limped with his left foot."*

The camera turns to the curved staircase. The door opens. The black angel comes out. He is shining. His hand lingers on the snow-covered railing. He limps with his left foot. After the last step, he walks towards the camera. This is all accompanied by the sound of the edge of a crystal bowl being rubbed by a wet finger.

The child. The angel, seen from behind, leans over the body.

We see the mechanism of his wings. It looks like the nervous system of a bee. He covers the child with his cloak.

The loges. The young woman is powdering her face. An older woman sleeps. Her husband, a man with a white beard, touches her shoulder. She straightens herself up, with a haggard face. The large woman smiles and replies to waves from the audience.

The angel. He is stretched out flat on his stomach on the cloak. This is accompanied by the sound of an airplane engine that gets louder and louder, splutters and roars, devastating the silence.

Accompanied by this din, the camera turns to the gas lamp and then to the loges with their chattering occupants.

The author's voice: *"The cloak, spread out like an ink stain, disappeared under the body of the supernatural being, who grew paler as he absorbed his prey."*

Negative shot of the angel. Huge, spread out, sprawling on the pale cloak, he turns back towards the loges with the look of a dying animal.

The noise of the engine reaches its climax.

It fades away as the camera frames the loges. Finally it stops and the indistinct and silly chattering of the spectators can be heard.

The camera comes back to the table and then turns to the ground, where the shape of the child's body, which has disappeared, can be seen as a hollow in the snow.

The sound of the crystal bowl is heard again. Close-up of the

poet's hand holding his cards. The black hand of the angel comes down from the top of the screen, grabs the ace of hearts and takes it away.

The Louis XV friend watches this scene. He starts. His eyes follow the angel's departure.

The angel puts his hand on the railing of the curved stairway. He walks slowly up the steps. At the top he opens the door and, before disappearing, turns his head one last time towards the card table. He disappears.

Close-up of the young woman holding her cards. Her eyes and mouth show scorn. She speaks: *"If you don't have the ace of hearts, my dear, you're a lost man."*

Fade-out of the young woman. In front of her, the poet is looking at her and at his cards. The sound of his heart beating is heard, much as he hears it himself, and as he imagines others hear it. The lapels of his coat throb to its rhythm.

The camera passes behind the poet. Full-face shot of the young woman. She fixes her eyes on him. He turns away, no longer able to stand her gaze.

Profile shot of the table. The poet, under the gaze of the motionless woman, puts his hand in his pocket. He brings out a revolver, puts it to his right temple and shoots. Sound of the gun going off. He falls onto the snow-covered table.

The view from the other side of the table: Close-up of the poet's face. His left cheek is resting on the snow. The blood spurts from his right temple and flows capriciously onto his right cheek. It branches out, comes together and catches on his eyelashes, his nostrils, and the corners of his lips.

The loges. People applaud.

The Louis XV friend looks reproachfully towards the loges. The applause doubles.

The camera returns to the rivulets of blood that crisscross the poet's face.

A palm tree decorates the pedestal that the Louis XV friend is leaning against. Through the leaves we can see the loges where the intermission chatter has started again.

Profile shot of the table. The poet is lying there, with his face, invisible, turned towards the pedestal. One of his hands hangs down. The young woman stands up. She is wearing black gloves that reach the point where the statue's arms were broken off. She throws down her cards, and they scatter. At that moment her eyes become motionless, drawn in black on her eyelids.

The author's voice: *"Having achieved her purpose, the woman became a statue once more, or, in other words, an inhuman object with black gloves in contrast to the snow upon which her steps no longer leave a trace."*

The camera moves in closer up to the woman-statue and the Louis XV friend. At a signal from her, the taffeta cape leaves the friend's shoulder and covers hers. Walking like a sleep-walker, she goes off towards the entrance to the rue l'Amsterdam. As she passes the trellis wall at the corner of the house

with the curved stairway, a light metal ball moves slowly through space, from right to left. The woman-statue goes through the arch. The metal ball moves slowly through space from left to right, towards the spot where the student, Dargelos, threw his snowball.

The camera turns to a sumptuous sculptured golden door at the top of a few steps. To the right and the left of the door is the same terra-cotta bust of Diderot.

Solemn music. The two parts of the door open. The woman-statue is standing there. The blind actress (with eyes painted on her eyelids) takes a few careful steps, illuminated by an intense light. She stops at the edge of the first step. Her right

hand, in a black glove, holds back the hood of her cape, showing half of her profile which she turns from left to right, as she did at the card table.

This last pantomime is shot from the waist up.

Back view of the woman. She raises her hand. The doormen whistle, calling the cars. Lower down, on the right of the screen, a bull's head appears on the snow. The animal stands at the bottom of the stairs. The woman wraps herself up in her cloak and starts to go down.

The empty staircase.

The bull, led by the woman on its right. They appear to be walking only because the camera is retreating.

Another shot of the bull and the woman, lower down on the screen. Four pieces of a 'orn, dismembered map of Europe

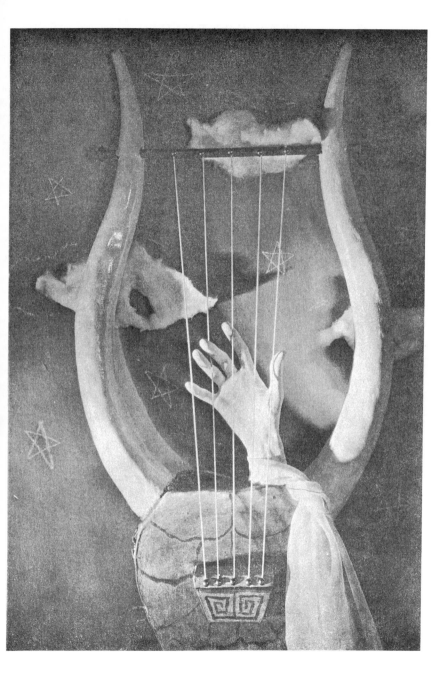

are stuck on the bull's cloak with cow-dung.

The empty screen on a black background. Whirling dust silvers the screen. The bull's horns appear on the bottom of the screen. Sound of a gong. The horns rise up the screen. They are a lyre.

The camera draws back. The bull and Europe have disappeared. Two stagehands are there, one standing on the other's shoulders, draped like the woman. The one on top is holding, in place of his face, a slate with a profile drawn in chalk on it.

The one underneath is holding the lyre and a globe of the world. This false woman, blending with the black background, except for the profile and the accessories, recedes into the phosphorescent night. She becomes smaller and smaller.

The author's voice: *"The road . . ."*

Fade-out. A close-up of the woman-statue's face, lying down. It is the actress's real face, but re-drawn in outline on her white skin in the author's style. Outline drawing of the hair on her bald head. Eyes closed.

The author's voice: *"... is long ..."*

Fade-out. A bird's-eye view of the woman-statue, lying down, an Acropolis of linen, of flowing draperies. The lyre and the globe are beside her.

Close-up of her face. Her mouth, drawn in relief, is half-open. Smoke comes out of it and rises.

Long shot again. The screen slowly darkens. Only the white surfaces, which become hard and stony and still hold the light, remain.

The author's voice: *"The mortal tedium of immortality."*

Cut. We see the crumbling factory chimney. After the noise of its collapse, the author's voice says:

The End

Postscript

(Text of the talk given at the Théâtre du Vieux-Colombier, when the film was shown there in January, 1932.)

It is somewhat ridiculous for me to be addressing an audience such as you. It would be better if I could speak every evening. As an audience, you are composed of people who guess words before they are spoken, and images before they are shown. But I will speak, as I have promised to do so.

First of all, I will give you an example of praise and of reprimand that I received. Here is the praise.

It comes from a woman who works for me. She asked me for tickets to the film, and I was foolish enough to fear her presence. I said to myself: "After she has seen the film, she won't want to work for me." But this is how she thanked me: "I saw your film. It's an hour spent in another world." That's good praise, isn't it?

And now the reprimand, from an American critic.

He reproaches me for using film as a sacred and lasting medium, like a painting or a book. He does not believe that film-making is an inferior art, but he believes, and quite rightly, that a reel goes quickly, that the public are looking above all for relaxation, that film is fragile and that it is pretentious to express the power of one's soul by such ephemeral and delicate means, that Charlie Chaplin's or Buster Keaton's first films can only be seen on very rare and badly spoiled prints. I add that the cinema is making daily progress and that eventually films that we consider marvelous today will soon be forgotten because of new dimensions and color. This is true. But for four weeks this film has been shown to audiences who have been so attentive, so eager and so warm, that I wonder after all if there is not an anonymous public who are looking for more than relaxation in the cinema. This same American critic congratulated me for inventing the "tragic gag." I did not invent the tragic gag, but I used it as much as possible. The gag is a great find. Here is an example. Charlie Chaplin swallows a whistle and all the dogs follow him. The audience bursts into laughter. With the tragic gag I don't expect the audience to laugh (if they do, I have failed) but I expect a black silence from them that is almost as violent as laughter.

I also want to tell you immediately about my luck. The cinema is exclusive. It cannot fall into the hands of the poets, or if it does, it demands the worst sacrifices from them. But I kept my freedom with this film. It is a unique case, and, if one likes this film, one must take that into consideration so that my part in it isn't over-glorified. With the film one can kill death, kill literature, and give life to the poetry of a direct existence. Imagine what the cinema of poets could be. But, alas, let me repeat that film-making is not an enterprise in which one can take risks.

In *The Blood of a Poet* I tried to film poetry the way that the Williamson brothers film the bottom of the sea. It meant letting down the diver's bell deep inside me, like the diver's bell they let down deep into the sea. It meant capturing the poetic state. Many people believe that this poetic state does not exist, that it's a sort of voluntary excitement. But even those who think they are the furthest away from the poetic state have known it. They only have to think of a great grief, or a great fatigue. They are curled up by the fire dozing, but they are not asleep. They immediately have associations that are not associations of ideas, or of images, or of memories. They are more like coupling monsters, secrets that emerge in the light, a whole equivocal and enigmatic world, quite capable of giving one an idea of the nightmare in which poets live, that makes their lives so moving, and that the public so wrongly interprets as exceptional exhilaration.

Of course, nothing is so hard as trying to get close to poetry. It is rather like wild animals. People complain that films about Africa are full of tricks. How could they not be? Filming lions and the roars of lions, and ending up with bedroom scenes and the sound of glasses forces our explorers to become artists, or, in other words, to give the illusion of what they have seen and heard, thanks to the bedroom scenes and the sound of glasses so expertly handled by the Hollywood specialists. I won't conceal the fact that I have used tricks in order to make poetry visible and audible. Here are some of them.

First you will see the poet go into a mirror. Then he swims in a·world that neither you nor I know, but that I have imagined. This mirror leads him to a corridor, and he moves as though he's in a dream. It is neither swimming nor flying. It's something else that isn't like anything else. Slow-motion is vulgar. So I nailed the sets onto the floor and filmed the scene from above. So the poet drags himself along instead of walking, and when the scene is put right again, you see a man walking very strangely with great effort, and the movements of his muscles do not correspond to the effort of his walk.

Miss Miller has pale eyes, but at some moments in my film she has dark eyes. I painted these eyes on her eyelids. I did not do it for aesthetic reasons, nor to make her look like a mask of Antinoe. I painted them because, when she is blind, she behaves as though she is blind and as one doesn't realize on the screen that her eyes are false, this behavior adds to the unreality of the character.

Another trick. I wanted to show the poet's statue being destroyed by the children who are playing, devastating everything, and respecting nothing. This stone statue has to disappear as though it were made of snow. This meant opposing this phenomenon with a very realistic scene, so as to achieve a contrast. I even replaced the real pure snow with Parisian slush — that gray mud that Paris children fight each other with and that is less photogenic and less attractive than Russian snow.

The public often mistakenly thinks that it is being made fun of by the artists. It's not possible. First of all, because the artist would have nothing to gain from it; and also because the particularly exhausting work of film-making is too absorbing for one to think of it. Thought is substituted by a sleepwalker's mechanism. Can you imagine the work involved in making a film? You arrive at dawn, the hour of the guillotine, and you go from studio to studio until midnight. You try hard not to ruin the company you are working for. You don't eat. You sleep standing up. You stagger around. After four days, unless you have a very strong American constitution, you're done for. You don't know where you are anymore. This is one of the reasons that film-making would be a very good poetic weapon. Sleeping on one's feet means talking without realizing it, confiding things. It means that you say things that you wouldn't tell anyone. You open up. The dark is no longer dark. The diver's bell that I spoke of starts off. This is why the film you are about to see is confessional, and as obscure as possible — in the sense that the spectators use the word "obscure."

Even if I wanted to tell you what happens in the film I would not be able to. People have said, even as a compliment, that the film lacks technique. That is not true. There is no film technique. There is the technique that each person discovers — you sink or swim. In the circumstances, you invent your own swimming style. I never had anything to do with film-making before. I was admirably supported and surrounded, and I don't accuse any of my collaborators of having left me in the lurch. I insisted on being alone so that I could discover the method that suited me. I just used to say to Périnal, "Périnal, I need decadent lighting here," or, "Périnal, I need funereal lighting here." He didn't answer. He just nodded and I got what I wanted. How can film-makers make so many films and remain calm? You ask yourself if you're going to live through to the end of the day. Miss Miller is an example. (My actors are remarkable because I didn't choose them for their physical beauty, but for their spiritual bearing. For in a film, the faces are immense and the eyes reveal everything.) Well, Miss Miller didn't realize that she was playing her role. She kept saying: "Is that me? Is that me? It's not possible!" All she remembered was sitting on a chair for hours, sleeping, fainting, eating sandwiches and drinking lukewarm beer. But I don't feel sorry for her and I don't regret anything. When a film is brilliantly organized the result is too precise, too polished, and unfashionable in very little time. I would prefer a wheelbarrow to a Rolls Royce because they keep changing shape and engine. Therefore, it isn't so bad to be a victim of the luxury of factories whose directors scorn poets. These directors have even helped me when they thought they were injuring me. One day they had their carpets beaten just to annoy me, but that is the dust that silvers the end of the film, and gives it a style of apotheosis.

As I said earlier, one can't tell the story of film like this. I could give you my own interpretation. I could say: the solitude of the poet is so great, he lives out his own creations, so vividly that the mouth of one of his creations is imprinted on his hand like a wound; that he loves this mouth, that he loves himself, in other words; that he wakes up in the morning with this mouth against him like a chance acquaintance; that he tries to get rid of it, that he gets rid of it, on a dead statue — that this statue comes to life — that it takes its revenge; that it sends him off into terrible adventures. I could tell you that the snowball fight represents the poet's childhood and that when he plays the card game with his Glory, with his Destiny, he cheats by drawing from his childhood instead of from within himself. I could tell you that afterwards, when he has tried to create a terrestrial glory for himself, he falls into that "mortal tedium of immortality" that one always dreams of when in front of famous tombs. I'd be right to tell you all that, but I'd also be wrong, for it would be a text written after the images. And anyway, are these images images? Life creates great images without realizing it. The drama on Calvary did not take place for the benefit of painters. When I was working, let me say again, I wasn't thinking of anything, and this is why one must let the film act like Auric's noble accompanying music. Music gives nameless nourishment to our emotions and memories, and if each of you find your own personal meaning in this film, then I will have achieved my ambition.

Let me add that three sequences have caused serious misunderstandings. First, one of the headings:

"The Profanation of the Host." I remember that this is borrowed from a painting by Paolo Ucello that was shown in an Italian exhibition in London.

Then the bleeding child. I believed that one does not distort space in films, and that films exhaust us with faces shot from above or from below. I wanted to shoot my film from directly in front, without artifice. But if the cinema forbids distortions in space, it allows distortions in time. A story from my childhood still haunts me. It can be found in some of my works. A young boy wounded by a snowball. In *Les Enfants Terribles* the child does not die. In my film, the child dies. I am not reworking a theme. It is a whole mythology that the poet stirs up and examines from different angles. The bleeding child, in reality, had a nose-bleed and bled very little. As I remember it, he was choking with blood. However, I didn't want to film a realistic scene, but the distorted memory of this scene.

Then there are the people in the loges who are applauding, but not the dead child, as some people seemed to think. The child is carried away by the angel when the loges applaud and it is the poet killing himself whom they are applauding. Poets, in order to live must often die, and shed not only the red blood of their hearts, but the white blood of their souls, that flows and leaves traces which can be followed. That is the price of applause. Poets must give their all in order to obtain the slightest approval.

To end this improvisation, for which I apologize, I will tell you that the poet is very unskilled when he speaks, as he is awoken from the sleep in which he composes his works. It is like a medium speaking out of a trance. The poet's work detests and devours him. There isn't room for both the poet and his work. The work profits from the poet. Only after his death can the poet profit from the work. And anyway, the public prefer dead poets and they are right. A poet who isn't dead is an anachronism. And so as not to present you with such a monstrous spectacle, I shall now give way to a form of myself, that may be obscure and painful, but that is a thousand times more real than the one that you hear and see now.[1]

[1] Text taken down in shorthand word for word. The author feels that he should not correct any mistakes that he may have made, any more than he should correct any mistakes in the scenario.

The Testament of Orpheus

"The tragedy of poets is that they must live
beyond the means of their era."   J.C.

Preface

A man who dozes, his mouth half open, in front of a wood fire, lets slip some secrets from that night of the human body that is called the soul, over which he is no longer master.

The sentry of his mouth has fallen into a deep and imprudent sleep, and words escape that do not know the password.

The Testament of Orpheus is simply a machine for creating meanings. The film offers the viewer hieroglyphics that he can interpret as he pleases so as to quench his inquisitive thirst for Cartesianism.

(I have said in *The Potomak* that if a housewife were given a literary work of art to rearrange, the end result would be a dictionary.)

This film has nothing to do with dreams except that it borrows the rigorous illogicality of dreams, their way of giving during the night, a kind of freshness to the falsehoods of the day that is dulled by routine. In addition, it is realistic, if realism means a detailed painting of the intrigues of a universe that is personal to every artist and is totally unrelated to what we are used to accepting as reality. The film disobeys dead rules, paying homage to all who wish to remain free. It brings into play a form of logic that reason does not recognize. In short, it is Cartesian by means of anti-Cartesianism.

My first attempt of this kind was *The Blood of a Poet,* and that old film is still puzzling people everywhere. Exegesis, which is a Muse, is still examining it, and the psychoanalyst is discovering what the shadowy part of me unknowingly expressed long ago.

I later orchestrated this method with the film *Orpheus*. But, looking back I am convinced that there is quite a considerable public who wish to go beyond the plot and do not try to flee the obscure. On the contrary, they are able to find their way unafraid or else with an adorable childish fear.

This is why I am abandoning the career of film-maker. Technical progress has now brought that career within everyone's reach. The progress that interests me is of a different, interior kind. And I flatter myself that, thanks to my own long-ago research, I am no longer the only archaeologist of my darkness.

Jean Cocteau.

P.S. This film may be the first attempt at transmuting words into acts, at organizing these acts instead of organizing the words of a poem, at a syntax of images instead of a story accompanied by words.

No Symbols

When a Frenchman no longer understands he never asks himself if it is necessary to understand — he either gets angry or he takes refuge in symbols. "I don't understand, therefore it must be a symbol," is a typically French way of thinking. "Either what I'm seeing doesn't mean anything, or else it means something different from what I am seeing, and that something different may be hiding a symbolic meaning." For instance, while in Ibsen's *Peer Gynt* the realistic actions, through the intervention of the hero's imagination, sweep the play along with a procession of symbols and political allusions, my film, though at times it may be reminiscent of *Peer Gynt*, differs from it in that the mysterious actions that it presents are supposed to correspond to the ceremony of another world, but in fact correspond to nothing in our world, and above all, in my mind, to nothing that I wish to talk about on film.

Often, while making the film, I understood so little of what I was producing that I was tempted to call it absurd and to cut it out. At those times, I forced myself to condemn my own judgment and to tell myself that if the film wanted it that way to begin with, it must have had its reasons, or that reason had nothing to do with it. And I was content to obey.

The Film-Maker as a Hypnotist

The danger with films is that we get used to seeing them
without paying the same attention we would pay to a play or
a book. But it is a first-class vehicle of ideas and of poetry
that can take the viewer into realms that previously only sleep
and dreams had led him to. I have often thought that it would
be not only economical but admirable if a fakir were to hyp-
notize an entire auditorium. He could make his audience see
a marvelous show, and moreover could order them not to
forget it on waking. This, in a way, is the role of the screen —
to practice a kind of hypnotism on the public and enable a
large number of people to dream the same dream together.
This phenomenon is hard to achieve in France, where every
member of an individualistic crowd puts up an instinctive
resistance to what is offered him, and feels that the desire to
convince him is a rape of his personality.

The Original Sin of Art

I am too used to being bottom of the class to pretend to be first in anything whatsoever. It is not first place that I covet, but a place apart, however small. "He was of *another* kind, of *another* kind was his title of nobility," thus did I speak of Manolete, thus would I like to be spoken of one day.

The same goes for my film, *The Testament of Orpheus*. It does not claim to be an example, or to give a lesson in daring. Quite simply, I did not burden myself with any commercial idea, or with any of the cinematographic imperatives. A sniper I was born, a sniper I'll remain. And I want to thank all those who not only agreed to follow me, but who also encouraged me when the absurd control of intelligence made me afraid. They helped me to overcome my fears and never to make the slightest concession. It is probably due to the atmosphere of confidence that they created around me that the film owes its curious effectiveness — I notice its power on people who seem least likely to submit to this kind of hypnosis and penetrate into the realm of the unknown.

The original sin of art is that it wanted to convince and to please, like flowers that grow in the hopes of ending up in a vase. I made this film without expecting anything other than the profound joy that I felt in making it.

Whether this work meets with approval or disapproval, it remains just as true that no one in it seems to obey the rules of acting and that a Maria Casarès, a François Périer, a Jean Marais, a Yul Brynner, a Crémieux cannot be judged as actors, but, along with Madame Alec Weisweiller, the maître d'hôtel, Dermit or myself, as people to whom things happen, people who cannot depend in any way on any theatrical science. It is the resurrectional and, as Salvador Dali would say, the "phoenixological" quality of the film that makes it re-live at every showing episodes that it was not aware of the night before. Let me add that its economy comes not only from the generosity of the famous actors who co-operated with me, but also from their immediate fore-knowledge of what I expected from them.

The names of the protagonists do not appear in the credits, because, first of all, I did not want to profit, in terms of publicity, from the favor that they agreed to do me and, secondly, because some names might have tricked the public into hoping for more than just a brief appearance of their favorite stars.

Jean Cocteau.

PHOENIXOLOGY

Where will this tight-lipped dream go,
Where the world was in itself made mock of.
Where glory shone like a nocturnal sun
Haloing Minerva, false-faced.

We know those Mata-Haris
Toppling over into middle-age,
From an old masterpiece to a new, soon frescoes
Pinned to the wall by twelve young soldiers.

One foot on the earth locks the other in the dream.
Limping towards the call of Hell in Val des Baux
I enrich, through the holes of its funereal sponge
A night waiting for my choice of graves.

Credits

Script and Direction	Jean Cocteau
Technical assistant	Claude Pinoteau
Director of Photography	Roland Pontoizeau
Sets	Pierre Guffroy
Sound	Pierre Bertrand
	René Sarazin
Editing	Marie-Josèphe Yoyotte
Costumes and Sculptures	Janine Janet

Produced by Jean Thuiller *for Les Editions Cinégraphiques*

Cast

Jean Cocteau	*The Poet*
Jean-Pierre Léaud	*The Schoolboy*
Nicole Courcel	*The Young Mother*
Françoise Christophe	*The Nurse*
Henry Crémieux	*The Professor*
Daniel Gélin	*The Intern*
Philippe Juzau	*First Man-Horse*
Daniel Moosmann	*Second Man-Horse*
Alice Sapritche	*A Gypsy*
Marie-Josèphe Yoyotte	*A Gypsy*
Edouard Dermit	*Cegestius*
Maître Henry Torrès	*The Master of Ceremonies*
Michèle Comte	*The Little Girl*
Maria Casarès	*The Princess*
François Périer	*Heurtebise*
Madame Alec Weisweiller	*The Confused Lady*
Philippe	*Gustave*
Guy Dute	*First Man-Dog*
J.-C. Petìt	*Second Man-Dog*
Alice Heyliger	*Isolde*
Michèle Lemoig	*First Lover*
Gerard Chatelain	*Second Lover*

Yul Brynner   *The Court Usher*
Claudine Oger   *Minerva*
Jacqueline Picasso
Lucia Bosé
Pablo Picasso
Luis-Miguel Dominguin
Charles Aznavour
Serge Lifar
Jean Marais   *Oedipus*
Brigitte Morissan   *Antigone*

Before the credits, which do not bear the names of the actors, the last images from the film Orpheus *are projected.*

THE TESTAMENT OF ORPHEUS
or
"Do Not Ask Me Why"

After the credits I begin to draw Orpheus' profile in chalk on a blackboard.

I SPEAK: It is the film-maker's privilege to be able to allow a large number of people to dream the same dream together, and to show us, moreover, the optical illusions of unreality with the rigor of realism. In short, it is an admirable vehicle for poetry.

My film is nothing other than a striptease show, consisting of removing my body bit by bit and revealing my soul quite naked. For there is a considerable public interested in the world of shadows, starved for the more-real-than-reality, which one day will become the sign of our times.

Here is the legacy of a poet to the successive groups of people who have always supported him.

A tangle of smoke dissolves slowly and curls out through a soap bubble, that appears to have come out of the point of a knife.

My hand, the knife, the bubble leave the screen and give way to an empty studio where all the elements of the set will appear in succession.

We see a young boy sitting at a school desk. While he con-

83

tinues to write, the Poet, dressed in Louis XV style, appears and moves towards the desk, after throwing down his three-cornered hat which disappears into the distance.

COMMENTARY: As my hat was annoying me I have sent it back to that other distant time — from which I could escape for only a few minutes.

THE POET: I wish to speak to the Professor.

THE YOUNG BOY *(stunned):* What are you doing here?

THE POET: Nothing! Who are you? His son?

YOUNG BOY: My father was an architect and he's dead. It is I who'd like to become a famous professor. But that won't be just yet.

POET: Ah, fine . . .! *(He disappears)*

COMMENTARY: I had forgotten my gloves. I was going to have to scare the boy again.

Close up: The young boy's fright.

The Poet reappears to collect his gloves from the desk.

POET: Excuse me.

He disappears again.

YOUNG BOY: *(Stands up behind his desk and shouts):* Sir! Sir!

He disappears.

Another corner of the empty studio. A bench, a gas lamp, a baby carriage, give it the appearance of a public square. A

young mother of forty years ago is rocking a baby and shaking a rattle. The Poet appears and moves up behind the mother. He leans over her, she sees him, cries out in fright, and drops the baby who falls to the ground.

THE POET'S VOICE: Charming!

He snaps his fingers and disappears.

The mother picks up the screaming child. She puts it in the pram and rushes out between the studio projectors.

COMMENTARY: This was my second meeting with a person whose destiny, against all logic, I had muddled.

A third corner of the empty studio. A long strip of carpet at the end of which we see a nurse pushing an old man in a wheelchair. We hear the Poet (still invisible) sniff as he takes a pinch of snuff. The nurse stops, and the poet appears, his handkerchief in his hand. The nurse draws back, terrified.

POET: Do not be afraid, Miss. My costume is the result of a bet . . . Is that the Professor that you are pushing in that wheelchair?

NURSE: Yes, sir. But would you explain . . .

POET: Impossible. May I ask him a question?

NURSE: The Professor won't be able to hear or answer you. When he was a child his mother was scared by something . . .

(The Poet makes a comical grimace.)

and she dropped him on his head. He lived without suffering from the fall, but one day . . .

COMMENTARY: The Professor's life hung by a thread. It broke.

Close-up of the old man dying, his mouth open.

Another close-up of his hand dropping a little round box. The nurse, utterly terrified, retreats, pulling the wheelchair backwards without even noticing that the Professor is dead. We see the Poet's boot and his hand, as he kneels and picks up the box.

Box, hand and foot fade away and all that is left is a dusty footprint on the carpet.

COMMENTARY: At last I had it, this box that would free me. . . .
I stroked it lovingly.

Another part of the studio. Phials and test-tubes. The Professor (about fifty years old) enters, supported by an intern. They are both wearing white coats and caps. The Professor falls into a chair behind a huge table covered with scientific paraphernalia.

PROFESSOR: It's nothing. I'll close my eyes for a moment, and then I'll be able to continue our research.

INTERN: Would you like me to give you an injection, Professor?

PROFESSOR: No thanks. Leave me alone. I'll be better in a few minutes. It's because of that fall. You never know what effects these stupid accidents can have one day.

COMMENTARY: It is probably quite a different fall from the one the baby professor had, but the intemporal had just made me responsible for it.

The intern moves away and goes up a staircase that does not lead anywhere. This staircase is part of an old set that has been forgotten there.

Close-up of the Professor looking very unwell. A hand appears on his shoulder. He lifts up his head and sees the Poet's face, with a Louis XV wig.

POET: Hello. Don't you recognize me?

PROFESSOR: I believe I . . .

POET: Try.

PROFESSOR: Aren't you the strange person who appeared to me during my youth?

POET: You've got it.

PROFESSOR: I was 13 . . . and I remember it as though it were yesterday. You frightened me terribly. . . . I would like to understand . . .

POET: Professor, you must be the only person in the world capable of not trying to understand and also capable of understanding what is not understandable. I wanted to know too much. I've been most imprudent. Now I'm paying for it. Now I am lost in space-time. I was looking for you, not without some difficulty. This costume is not a theatrical one. It is the costume of the period that I was taken to by a dangerous escapade. What year is this?

PROFESSOR: 1959.

POET: My God! If my calculations are correct we should be in the year 2209 . . .

PROFESSOR: I would no longer be alive . . .

POET: Professor Langevin . . .

PROFESSOR *(while the Poet walks round the table):*
Like all scholars, Professor Langevin was most naïve. Only the nineteenth century believed that there was such a thing as precise sciences. Professor Langevin did not know that the perspectives of time obey the same laws as the perspectives of space. It is true that 250 years have passed since you left. But your return cancels them out, and those 250 years do not concern either of us. May I ask you how you managed to travel through time?

POET *(In a different part of the studio):*
Poets know quite a few ... awesome things.

PROFESSOR: I sometimes think they know far more than we do.

POET: Professor, it is difficult to explain the intemporal and even more so to live in it. One gets confused. Think of it: I have just seen you at different stages of your life, in rapid succession, without any chronological order. I have even known you when you were very old, just a few moments ago, my dear Professor. Your sick hand let this box fall. I took it, and by picking it up I believe I have done us both a favor.

He comes nearer the Professor, takes the box out of his pocket, and gives it to him.

PROFESSOR'S VOICE *(opening the box that is filled with bullets):*
This is admirable. It proves that you are not a fraud, and that I'll succeed in overcoming the obstacles that are exhausting me. But, alas, I suspect that it will no longer be possible for me to make my discovery known. Without you, it would still be in the hands of a sick man, and would die with me. Am I wrong? Most admirable. . . .

(The Professor looks right and left, then, in a low voice, as though afraid of being overheard):

> But tell me, dear Sir, man to man, do I die in your presence?

POET *(bowing from the waist, with a flourish of his riding whip):*
Forgive me, Professor, I have a very bad memory of the future.

PROFESSOR: Do you know the properties of these bullets?

POET: Yes. At first glance they are deceptive.

PROFESSOR: The powder is the only thing that counts.

POET: It's because of your bullets that I am looking for you through this frightful muddle of time and space. If I am not mistaken, they travel faster than light. Professor, I would like to be your guinea pig. It's my last hope. The only way I can go home.

PROFESSOR: Do you have a revolver?

POET: You forget that the only thing I can offer you is a horse pistol.

PROFESSOR: What could I have been thinking of? I have just what we need in a drawer. Scholars must be armed nowadays. Do you smoke?

POET: I won't say no.

(The Professor gives him a light.)

> To be able to smoke in 1770 I had to pretend to invent

the cigarette. They told me it was a ridiculous invention and that it hadn't a chance of succeeding.

PROFESSOR: You are aware of how my experiment is to proceed. First of all I'll have to kill you.

POET: Relatively speaking?

PROFESSOR: Relatively speaking.

POET: Are you sure it will work?

PROFESSOR: No doubt at all. I shall unfold a fold in time. Everything that you have just lived will be wiped out, like figures from a blackboard.

Back view of the Poet walking towards the studio's big sliding door. He stops, turns round, throws his cigarette far away and raises his riding whip.

POET: I know the score.

PROFESSOR: Then don't be afraid. Are you ready?

POET *(slashing the air with his riding whip):* Fire!

The Poet falls off-screen and stands up immediately, wearing modern dress, which he keeps throughout the whole film. He moves like a sleepwalker towards the big door.

COMMENTARY: The Professor was too clever not to realize that it wasn't enough for me to change my clothes in order to move back into our time and to live in it in flesh and blood.

The Poet opens the sliding door. It is evening. The Victorine studios. The Professor appears on the step of the big door and waves good-bye.

PROFESSOR: Good luck!

POET: I really owe you something!

PROFESSOR: Remember, I won't answer for whatever may happen from now on . . .

POET: Those are risks we have to take.

Music: Handel.

The Poet walks off, while the Professor closes the door, on which a tall studio crane projects its shadow.

Front view of the Poet who is still walking like a sleepwalker on a road in Les Baux de Provence. He passes the man-horse, a young man in a black leotard with a long black horse's tail, and a horse's head and neck over his own. The man-horse stops, turns round and takes off his mask. He has the face of a gypsy and watches gravely as the poet walks away.

After he has put the mask back on, the Poet turns round and retraces his steps, behind the man-horse.

This slow pursuit leads him into a sort of tall Egyptian tomb, where the man-horse disappears between the chalky blocks.

The Poet also goes in, and walks along a wall, like the walls of childhood dreams.

We hear the far-off rhythm of flamenco guitars, which slowly becomes louder and louder, until it is deafening; a group of young people is playing.

The gypsy camp. The gypsies put up camp in a sort of circle of rocks. The Poet approaches them cautiously. The man-horse, sitting on the steps of a caravan, is combing his mane,

the mask resting on his knees. The flamenco music becomes softer and gives way to the sound of the comb. A little further, a young gypsy girl takes the soup off the fire. In the flames the photograph of Cegestius in Orpheus *materializes. The photograph, rolled up, leaps into her hands. She unrolls it, looks at it and takes it to a gypsy woman sitting at a little table, who is smoking and reading cards. The gypsy girl takes the photograph and tears it into pieces which she holds out to the Poet, who has now reached the table. The Poet, holding the pieces of the photograph in his hand, retreats from the gypsy camp. The man-horse stands up and watches him leave.*

COMMENTARY: I recognized from afar the photo of Cegestius, one of the last shots from my film *Orpheus*. I did not like that man-horse. I guessed that he was drawing me into a trap, and that I would have been wiser not to follow him.

(The Poet walks down the smuggler's path that leads to the Saint-Jean lighthouse.)

Fate led me to believe that I was about to do something imprudent . . . throw Cegestius' torn photo into the sea.

He throws the pieces of the photograph into the sea. At once a monstrous flower of foam is churned up, from which Cegestius issues like a stamen, flies up and lands gently on the shore, in front of the Poet, to whom he gives the Hibiscus flower. Dialogue, under the flashing beam of the lighthouse.

POET: Cegestius!

CEGESTIUS: You gave me my name. . . .

POET: I can hardly recognize you. You used to be blonde.

CEGESTIUS: That was for a film. This time it's no longer a film. It's life.

POET: You were dead.

CEGESTIUS: Just like everyone else.

POET: Why do you come back from the sea?

CEGESTIUS: Why. Always why. You try too hard to understand. It's a very serious fault.

POET: I've already heard that sentence.

CEGESTIUS: You wrote it. Take this flower. . . .

POET: But that flower is dead!

CEGESTIUS: Aren't you an expert in phoenixology?

POET: What's that?

CEGESTIUS: It is the science that allows one to die many times only to be reborn.

POET: I don't like that dead flower.

CEGESTIUS: One doesn't always revive what one likes. Let's go . . .

POET: Where are we going?

CEGESTIUS: Stop asking me questions.

They walk up the slope towards the lighthouse. It is dusk.

The beam lights up my tapestry of Judith and Holophernes.

Sound of trumpets.

COMMENTARY: Judith has just cut off the head of Nebuchad-
nezzar's captain, Holophernes.... The servant girl is
hovering on the doorstep of the room where the de-
capitation took place. Judith is no longer a woman,
the daughter of a rich Jewish banker; from now on she
is the sarcophagus that contains her own legend. It is
in that form that, in the moonlight, she moves through
the group of sleeping guards.

*Studio. A platform in front of the tapestry. A little girl,
dressed in her best clothes, jumps up onto the platform and
greets the master of ceremonies.*

M.C. *(sitting at his table):*
And now, listen carefully! Who, in antiquity, wove and
rewove her tapestry?

LITTLE GIRL: Penelope.

M.C.: Well done. And who was Penelope?

LITTLE GIRL: Penelope was the last ordeal that Ulysses had to
undergo at the end of his journey.

M.C.: Very good. And what does this tapestry represent?

LITTLE GIRL: Judith and Holophernes.

M.C.: And who designed it?

LITTLE GIRL: Jean Cocteau.

M.C.: And who is Jean Cocteau?

LITTLE GIRL *(unsure):* He plays in an orchestra?

M.C.: Quite right. And what instrument does he play?

LITTLE GIRL *(looking towards the ceiling):*
   A . . . a . . .

M.C.: A b . . . a ba . . .

LITTLE GIRL: A buffoon!

M.C.: No, not a buffoon, a bassoon. Well let's have lots of
   applause for our young candidate . . .

The master of ceremonies applauds.

*The little girl bows to an imaginary audience, while the Poet
and Cegestius pass behind her on the platform, toward the
right. The Poet holds the Hibiscus flower in his hand. Ceges-
tius guides him, without touching him. The little girl leaves
the studio, which now looks like the wings of a theatre.*

A garden. Evening sun.

The Poet and Cegestius go towards a greenhouse.

CEGESTIUS: We must hurry. The evening cocks are crowing.

*The greenhouse. We can see the outlines of an easel under a
large sheet and a stand where the model seems to be an empty
flowerpot. Cegestius' hand holds the Poet by the wrist and
makes him put the Hibiscus on the rim of the empty flowerpot.*

CEGESTIUS: Turn your night into day. Then we'll see who is
   giving the orders and who is carrying them out.

The Poet picks up a sheaf of paint brushes and walks up to

*the easel. The sheet ripples, flies off, and reveals a large paint-
ing: "Oedipus and his Daughters."*

*The action is repeated, the sheet flies off. A slightly smaller
painting: "Head of the dead Orpheus."*

COMMENTARY: Of course works of art create themselves, and
dream of killing both father and mother. Of course
they exist before the artist discovers them. But it's al-
ways "Orpheus," always "Oedipus." I thought that by
changing castle I'd change ghosts and that here a flower
could make them flee.

*The sheet hiding the last painting flies off, revealing a black-
board. The Poet wipes it with a rag, looking first at the flower-
pot then at the blackboard, as though he were drawing the
Hibiscus. A self-portrait of the Poet emerges from the rag.
The Poet draws back and throws down the paint brushes in
anger.*

Cegestius has put a skull mask over his face.

He speaks from behind it:

CEGESTIUS: Don't try any more, a painter always paints his own
portrait. You'll never succeed in painting that flower.

*The Poet grabs the Hibiscus, tears off the petals, tramples on
them and crushes them underfoot.*

POET: Damn! Damn! Damn! Damn! Damn!

CEGESTIUS (*picks up the remains of the flower as though they
were relics and puts them in the flowerpot):*
Aren't you ashamed of yourself?

They leave the greenhouse and arrive at the patio of the villa

Santo Sospir, decorated with my mosaics.

Cegestius puts the flowerpot on a table in front of the mosaic of the Satyr and moves away, giving way to the Poet.

The Poet is standing behind the table, wearing a gown and mortar-board. He sits down.

CEGESTIUS: Your turn, Professor. Show us what you can do.

Long silent scene, with music, Bach's Minuet and Badinerie. The camera frames the Poet's hands. These hands pull out what is left of the petals from the flowerpot and recreate the flower. He finishes his magic work by putting the stamen in place.

CEGESTIUS: Let's go.

POET *(without the gown and mortar-board):*
    Where are you taking me?

CEGESTIUS: To the Goddess.

POET: Which goddess?

CEGESTIUS: Some call her Pallas Athenae, some Minerva — and she doesn't go for fun and games, let me tell you.

POET: And if I refuse?

CEGESTIUS: Those are your orders. I don't advise you to disobey them.

POET: And the flower?

CEGESTIUS: Take it to her. Goddesses are women and women don't dislike being offered flowers.

POET: I won't go.

CEGESTIUS: You left me alone in that zone where the living are not alive and the dead are not dead.

(Said backwards)

> Have you ever wondered what would happen to me after Heurtebise and the Princess were arrested? Did you stop to think that you were leaving me alone in such a place?

(Speaking normally)

> Obey.

POET: I will obey.

They disappear through the gate of the villa.

Huge empty studio. There is a path of wooden boards crossing the whole length of the studio, ending at a door with three steps.

The Poet and Cegestius follow this path, go through the door and down the steps.

At that moment, not far from the steps, the Princess and Huertebise rise up onto the screen, seated at a long table, like the judges in the film Orpheus.

Chairs and documents appear at the same time.

The Poet, who had come down the steps, backs up them when the Princess and Heurtebise appear, accompanied by a sound like a sonic boom.

Cegestius remains at the top of the stairs, the Poet goes down them again, slowly. He walks towards the table, and recognizing the actors from his film Orpheus, *he smiles.*

POET: Hey!

PRINCESS *(coldly):* Hey, what?

POET: Forgive me. I'm being fooled by an extraordinary resemblance . . . what are you doing here?

PRINCESS: I'm the one that asks the questions. We are the inquiry commission of a tribunal to whom you must account for some of your acts. This tribunal wishes to know if you plead guilty or not guilty. *(To Heurtebise)* Would you read out the two accusations.

HEURTEBISE *(standing, holding documents in his hand):*

First: You are accused of innocence — or in other words, of an attack on justice by being capable and guilty of all crimes, instead of just one, and liable to be convicted in a way that our jurisdiction will decide. Second: You are accused of incessantly wanting to penetrate with fraudulence, into a world that is not yours. Do you plead guilty or not guilty?

POET: I plead guilty in the first and second instances. I admit that I am closed in by the threat of mistakes I have not made, and I admit that I have often wanted to jump over the fourth mysterious wall that men write their loves and dreams upon.

PRINCESS: Why?

POET: Probably because I am tired of the world I live in and detest habits. Also because of that disobedience with which audacity defies the rules, and that spirit of creation which is the highest form of the spirit of contradiction — pertaining to human beings.

PRINCESS: If I am not mistaken, you are making a religion out of disobedience?

POET: Without disobedience what would children do? or heroes? or artists?

HEURTEBISE: They would have to rely on their lucky stars.

PRINCESS: We are not here in order to attend oratorical joust-
ing matches. Put that flower on the table.

The Poet puts down the flower, which disappears.

PRINCESS: Where did you get that flower from?

POET: Cegestius gave it to me.

HEURTEBISE: Cegestius.... If I'm not mistaken that is the name
of a temple in Sicily.

POET: It's also the name of a young poet in my film *Orpheus.*
At first it was the name of one of the angels in my poem
"The Angel Heurtebise."

PRINCESS: What do you mean by "film"?

POET: A film is a petrifying source of thought. A film revives
dead acts — A film allows one to give a semblance of
reality to unreality.

PRINCESS: And what do you call unreality?

POET: What goes beyond our meager limits.

HEURTEBISE: So in your world there are individuals that are
like an invalid with no arms or legs, who sleeps, dream-
ing that he is moving and running.

POET: You have given an excellent definition of the poet.

PRINCESS: What do you mean by poet?

POET: The poet, by composing poems, uses a language that is neither dead nor living, that few people speak, and few people understand.

PRINCESS: And why do these people speak this language?

POET: To meet their compatriots in a world where, too often, the exhibitionism that consists of revealing one's naked soul is practiced only among the blind.

HEURTEBISE: Cegestius!

CEGESTIUS (from the steps where he is sitting, waiting for his turn to appear before the tribunal):
Present.

PRINCESS: Who are you?

CEGESTIUS (moving towards the table): This man's adopted son. My real name is Edward. I am a painter.

PRINCESS: He maintains that you are a poet named Cegestius.

HEURTEBISE: Is the name Cegestius a nickname?

POET: A pseudonym would be more correct.

HEURTEBISE: Your French language is most subtle.

PRINCESS: Did you not, a few terrestrial minutes ago, use an idiom that you have no right to use in this world?

CEGESTIUS: It's true. I gave in to a moment of anger, and I apologize.

PRINCESS: Don't do it again. What gave you the right to appear to this man and bring him this flower?

CEGESTIUS: The flower was dead. I had orders to give it to him so that he could revive it.

PRINCESS: Can you give me proof of your powers?

HEURTEBISE: And don't think we'll be convinced if you just vanish.

POET: Vanishing is not easy, though.

HEURTEBISE: No easier than the phenomenon that makes lovers so self-effacing before the object of their love.

PRINCESS: You're losing your head!

HEURTEBISE: I'm sorry. Sometimes I'm up in the clouds.

PRINCESS: I advise you not to make stupid and unsubtle jokes about matters that could enlighten men as to the vanity of what they undertake.

HEURTEBISE: We have nothing to fear from that point of view. We asked you to give us proof of your powers.

CEGESTIUS: I agree with this man when he declares that everything that can be proved is vulgar. I'm afraid you'll just have to take my word for it.

PRINCESS: Do you dare preach to me? That's really too much. I shall remember that.

(To the Poet)

Sir!

POET: I am listening.

PRINCESS: Did you write:
> "This body that contains us does not know ours.
> What lives in us is lived in.
> And these bodies, one inside the other
> Form the body of eternity."

POET: I wrote that, yes.

PRINCESS: And who told you these things?

POET: What things?

PRINCESS: The things that you say in that language that is neither dead nor living.

POET: No one.

PRINCESS: You are lying!

POET: I agree if, like myself, you believe that we are the servants of an unknown force that lives within us, manipulates us, and dictates this language to us.

HEURTEBISE *(in a low voice, leaning towards the Princess)*: He may well be an idiot....

PRINCESS *(in the same way, to Heurtebise)*: There is less to fear from intellectuals.

POET: Mascarille and Leporello passed themselves off as their masters. The poet is somewhat like them.

PRINCESS: Stop chatting, and don't speak unless I ask you to.

POET: I was only explaining, in all humility.

HEURTEBISE: We are not asking you to be either humble or proud. We are asking you to answer when you are questioned. That's all. Do not forget that you are a nocturnal amalgamation of caves, forests, marshes, red rivers, populated with huge and fabulous beasts who devour each other. It's nothing to show off about.

PRINCESS: Where do you live?

POET: I am the guest of a friend here.

PRINCESS *(close-up of her eyes):*
What are you talking about? There is no "here" where we are.

HEURTEBISE *(close-up of his eyes):*
We are not anywhere.

POET: But I have just passed in front of some mosaics and a tapestry that I designed and that decorate the villa I mentioned.

The Princess's hands tap impatiently on the table.

PRINCESS: It is possible that you passed in front of that tapestry and those mosaics, but only because we wanted to place that tapestry and those mosaics in your path. It doesn't matter where your gullible imagination places them. Please bring in the witness.

The Professor appears in the studio, wearing pyjamas and slippers.

PROFESSOR: Where am I?

HEURTEBISE: Now Professor, there's a sentence unworthy of a scientist. It's the sentence of a pretty woman who pretends to have fainted and come round.

PROFESSOR *(very vague):* I was in bed . . . I was sleeping . . .

PRINCESS *(smiling):* You are in bed, Professor, you are sleeping. But you are not dreaming. You are living in one of those folds of time that you have been studying. A study that does honor to your intelligence but that our reign does not approve of. You will wake up and you will remember us as though we were people in your dream.

(Pointing at the poet with her cigarette holder)

Do you know this man?

(The Professor puts on his glasses)

POET: Professor! You have a short memory. Of course your excuse is that you are sleeping. Did you not recently deprive me of my Louis XV cocoon — cloak, boots, ruffles, powdered wig, three-cornered hat, neckerchief?

PROFESSOR: But of course!

POET: I am not blaming you. You warned me quite honestly that you would not answer for whatever followed.

PROFESSOR: But what are you doing here?

PRINCESS *(calling him to order by tapping on the table):* Let me remind you again, gentlemen, that I am in charge here. I would be most grateful if you would keep quiet and answer my questions only. In what circumstances did you meet this man?

POET: That's one way of looking at it...

PROFESSOR: It's very simple....

HEURTEBISE: Silence!

PRINCESS: Answer.

PROFESSOR *(almost as though he were lecturing):*
> I was despairing of ever completing the important dis-
> covery of a method for achieving resurrection; and it
> is most likely that my discovery would have died with
> me had not this man, who is gifted with powers that I
> am ignorant of — powers that are related to chronons
> and particles of time — had not left our continuum to
> travel in the intemporal, had not got lost there, and
> brought me, from my future into my present, proof of
> my tardy success. I tried the experiment on him. I
> would like to add that, for fear of losing the respect of
> my colleagues at the Institute, I threw my discovery
> out of the window into the Seine, a river that flows past
> my house.

PRINCESS: So you accomplished a real tour-de-force — you re-
turned a man who was lost in time to his own period?

PROFESSOR: Exactly. I released him from the trap that his dan-
gerous attempt had caused him to fall into.

POET: Only to make me fall into another trap, Professor. Surely
that twilight that is neither night nor day, that I have
been walking through since I left your laboratory, can-
not be called living.

PROFESSOR: I deeply regret it. Alas, it is possible that my dis-
covery was not really perfect. That makes me even

more pleased that I have destroyed it.

HEURTEBISE: What form did your discovery take?

PROFESSOR: A box of bullets that my powder propels faster than light. That was the box that I threw into the river.

HEURTEBISE: Let's hope it won't cause unpleasant mutations. In any case it was a wise thing to do.

PRINCESS: The arrogant men who disrupt measures — even if they are clumsy ones — that your world adopted over a long period of time as a defense against its original disorder are taking a very great risk of breaking a chain in order to have an illusion of progress.

PROFESSOR: Madam! You are condemning the whole of science.

HEURTEBISE: What you call science. For there is a science of the soul that men worry very little about.

PRINCESS: Please, I beg you. . . .

HEURTEBISE: Excuse me.

PRINCESS: What could you say if you had to defend this man?

PROFESSOR: That he is a poet, or, in other words, that he is indispensable, although I know not to whom. May I ask you a question, Madam?

PRINCESS: We'll see if I am in a position to answer you.

PROFESSOR: Just the curiosity of a man of science — Just this: what time is it?

HEURTEBISE: No time, Professor, no time at all. Carry on sleeping. You are free.

PROFESSOR: Thank you. I feel . . . it's difficult to . . . a kind of tiredness . . . I think that . . .

HEURTEBISE *(very gently):*
Sleep . . . sleep, Professor. I want you to.

PROFESSOR: Thank you. Madam . . . my respects.

(As he disappears into the background)

I am sleeping.

PRINCESS *(with sarcasm):* Sleep well.

(To the Poet)

I am aware that the detours on your road are a sort of labyrinth — quite different from ours although they intermingle — and that although you were able to find the only person who could correct your mistakes and your disobedience of terrestrial laws, this was not because of absent-mindedness on the part of the unknown, but because of a kind of supreme indulgence that you abuse, dear Sir, and that could well betray you one day. However, if I am overstepping my limits here, it is because I wanted to warn you before consulting your guide about the extent of his privileges and responsibilities.

POET: I find it difficult to understand you.

HEURTEBISE: We are not asking you to understand.

PRINCESS: Stop playing the village idiot. I think you under-
stand perfectly and that you prefer to play the fool
rather than admit things.

POET: But, Madam . . .

HEURTEBISE: Silence. You should be glad of the incredible leni-
ency that the preventive tribunal has shown you.

PRINCESS: *(to Cegestius)* Come closer.
Yes . . . you . . . you . . .
Are you sure you haven't abused your own master so
that you could fuse your own two personalities — that
are dividing you — and because you did not like being
two people? Were you not tempted to become one per-
son, serving the foolish actions of this man, who also
has two roles — that of your real father and that of
your adoptive father?

CEGESTIUS: Madam, you must surely know of the terrible in-
finity of realms and orders, and that it often prevents
one from understanding which persons should obey
others and which should be obeyed.

PRINCESS: I grant you that. We will see about that. Could you
explain the strange road that you took in order to
appear to him?

CEGESTIUS: That road, which passed through fire and water,
was, I presume, the result of imperatives of which I am
but the instrument, and that go far beyond my weak
competence.

PRINCESS: Since you will persist in this attitude, I would at least
like to know what is the extent, here below, of your
powers of metamorphosis.

Cegestius grimaces.

> Oh! There's no need to look like that! I am referring
> to the metamorphosis of an orchid into a skull. That
> childish and macabre masquerade corresponded if I am
> not mistaken, to resurrectional phenomena. Was your
> only aim to impress this man, or was it a way of warning
> him?

CEGESTIUS: No. That rite was part of a ceremony that I do not
have the right to enlarge upon.

PRINCESS: The accused refuses to answer. Take note of that.

(To the Poet)

> Do you have anything to add in your defense?

POET: I would like to say that if I deserve punishment I cannot
imagine any more painful one than being forced to live
between two worlds, or to use your own words, between
two realms. A film-maker would say "through a colored
filter." I'd give anything to be able to walk on solid
ground again, and not to be lost in the shadows of a
strange universe.

PRINCESS: This is not within our jurisdiction. The tribunal
will determine it.

(She stands up, gathering up her papers.)

> The board of inquiry condemns you to the life sentence.

(She disappears slowly.)

HEURTEBISE: That's the minimum, especially at your age.

(He brings out the flower that he had kept hidden, and gives it to the Poet.)

Your flower.

POET: Heurtebise!

HEURTEBISE: Shh!

POET *(in a low voice):* And what about the Princess?

HEURTEBISE *(walking towards the door with the Poet):*
You know that, being in love with a mortal, she claimed to have transgressed the human laws of time....

POET: And Orpheus?

HEURTEBISE: His survival was a mirage. His divine head died and Eurydice was sent back to hell. A great man once said, "One must never spit into the wind." Take the flower.

POET: I don't dare take it.

HEURTEBISE: This isn't the first or the last time that I take this flower away from you and give it back to you.

POET: But this time I understand the courage of your gesture, and that I may cause you both to be condemned again, she and you....

HEURTEBISE: We couldn't be condemned to anything worse.

POET: What have you been condemned to?

HEURTEBISE *(disappearing):*
> To judging others. To being judges.

Long silence.

CEGESTIUS: That's unpleasant.

POET: Cegestius, that court of inquiry seemed very suspect to me. Our works dream only of killing both father and mother — in the person of ourselves — and of being free. But the creatures of our mind remain curious about their origins ... I wonder ...

He goes through the door.

CEGESTIUS: Don't wonder anything. It's better that way.

POET: I wonder if you yourself....

CEGESTIUS: It's possible. Sometimes I blame you for abandoning me in the zone of shadows. Sometimes I am pleased to live outside the absurd world that I used to live in. In spite of my revolts, I would like to rescue you from the dilemma you are in. However, although the zone ignores yesterday, today and tomorrow, your human state is subject to them, and in order to reach my goal, I must guide you, or rather follow you through unavoidable trials, only at the end of which I obtain what I want.

POET: Could you not enlarge on your role and the trials that await me?

CEGESTIUS: No. I don't know myself. I am in the dark. The only thing I know is that that flower is made from your blood, and has adopted the same rhythms as your destiny. Let's go. I've already said too much. Just be happy to obey.

POET *(in the same way as on the patio with the mosaics):*
I will obey....

Wide shot of the empty studio seen from the flies. The Poet and Cegestius cross it on the path of boards and disappear down a staircase that was not there previously.

The tapestry.

Cegestius and the Poet cross the platform, from right to left.

The garden in front of the villa Santo Sospir. A lady, wearing a dress from the Impressionistic period, in the manner of the young Sarah Bernhardt, walks round a fish-pond and stops. She is carrying a Japanese parasol and a paperback murder mystery. She raises her head and calls.

LADY: Gustave! Gustave!

THE MAITRE D'HOTEL *(he appears on the terrace):*
Your ladyship?

LADY *(tapping the open book with the bamboo handle of her parasol):*
Who is the murderer?

MAITRE D': I do not know, your ladyship.

LADY: It's incredible. Are you going to force me to read an entire book that won't appear for another seventy years?

MAITRE D': Please excuse me, your ladyship.

LADY: I am not interested in your excuses.

The Poet and Cegestius come down the staircase that leads from the terrace to the garden.

Who are these gentlemen?

MAITRE D': Which gentlemen, your ladyship?

LADY: Those two strange gentlemen who are walking around on my property.

MAITRE D': I don't see anyone, your ladyship.

LADY: It's too much! Are you saying I am crazy?

MAITRE D': Oh, your ladyship!

LADY: You may go. What strange times these are!

The Maître d' disappears, with bent shoulders. The lady blows a whistle that is hanging round her neck. The long sad whistle of a train at dusk is heard.

LADY: I must say, everything is topsy-turvy today.

Two young swimmers at the end of the garden. At the sound of the second whistle, the first swimmer puts on a mask of Anubis, the other, who is wearing a dog's tail, leans over and holds his companion by the hips, so that they simulate a dog.

The camera turns to the Poet and Cegestius at the foot of the stairs.

POET: Is that she?

CEGESTIUS: Don't be silly. That's a confused lady who is in the wrong era. You should be the first to know that these things can happen.

At the third whistle, the two swimmers, still like a dog, frisk about and pass behind the lady, who shrugs her shoulders and raises her eyes to the sky with an exasperated look. The lady and the dog disappear into the villa through a French window.

POET *(leaving the villa with Cegestius):*

What a strange dog!

A gate halfway down the hill, facing the sea. There is a notice on it that says: "Private Property, Traps."

The Hibiscus leaves the Poet's hand as though Heurtebise, invisible, had taken it from him.

The sound of Tristram's horn. The Poet and Cegestius go down the rocky steps that zigzag down to the sea.

The yacht, Orpheus II, with all sails out, crosses the screen from left to right.

The deck of the yacht. The Poet and Cegestius are sitting next to each other. They look back behind the boat.

The captain at the helm. On his left stands a woman in medieval dress.

POET: This time, is it she?

CEGESTIUS: No, that's Isolde. She is aboard all the ships in the world. She is looking for Tristram.

The camera comes back to the Poet and Cegestius. The harbor of Darse (Villefranche).

The Poet and Cegestius get out of a dinghy and disappear to the left.

They climb the steps in front of the Chapel of St. Peter.

COMMENTARY: It seems to me that I passed in front of the Chapel of St. Peter with Cegestius. I painted it in 1957 as my own sarcophagus, and gave it to the fishermen of Beaulieu and Saint-Jean, in memory of my dead youth, and to the fishermen of Villefranche where I lived for so long.

The arches that lead to the rue Obscure in Villefranche.

The rue Obscure.

The Poet and Cegestius pass the Poet's double, dressed differently from him.

His double turns round towards the Poet and Cegestius. The Poet turns round towards his double. Cegestius comes up to him.

CEGESTIUS: Well, what is it?

POET: Don't try to tell me you didn't see him.

CEGESTIUS: I saw him as clearly as I see you.

Dialogue as they walk on side by side.

POET: He pretended not to see me.

CEGESTIUS: You have said so many times that if you met him you wouldn't even want to shake his hand....

POET: He hates me.

CEGESTIUS: He has no reason to like you. He has been insulted and kicked around enough instead of you.

POET: I'll kill him.

CEGESTIUS: I don't advise you to. You may well be immortal, but if you kill him, you won't find anyone stupid enough to be killed instead of you.

POET: Where did he come from? Where's he going to?

CEGESTIUS: There you go, asking questions again. It's quite likely that he is going to where you have come from and that you are going to where he has come from. You spend your whole time trying to be, which prevents you from living. Come on now. The Gods don't like to be kept waiting.

End of Tristram's horn.

They go out through an air-vent and down a staircase of the manorial ruins of the village of Les Baux — the deserted road that leads down to the quarries. The Poet and Cegestius stop and listen to a faroff voice.

VOICE: I am the Key of Dreams. The sad column. The virgin with an iron mask.

POET: Is that she?

Cegestius bids him to follow. They enter the quarries.

We see them, very small, in the colossal nave of the quarries, where they have stopped. We hear the Poet's voice, but his lips do not move.

VOICE OF THE POET: It's your fault, Peloponnese. You are threatened by other dangers, for during the night, the statues put on black costumes and murder the travelers. But I, myself, I am not a statue. Tremble! I have enough sea in my veins to understand the language of the waves. By scrubbing and beating their washing on their knees they are insulting you, they are laughing, they are making fun of you.

Close-up of the Poet and Cegestius. Jazz music. We see what they see: A young couple in each other's arms. Each is writing down his impressions on a notebook on the other's back.

CEGESTIUS: Intellectual lovers. *(The Poet smiles.)*

A LITTLE BOY AND GIRL *(Running down the rocks and stopping in front of the young couple):*

Could we have your autographs?

(Which they are given.)

Thank you Sir, thank you Miss.

(The children run off.)

They come to the base of a statue amid geometrical ruins. On this base is an oracle in a long white robe. Its head is built of shells with several eyes and mouths. The children climb up an invisible ladder to these mouths and push in the autographs.

POET: What is that idol that eats autographs?

CEGESTIUS: It's a machine that will make anyone famous in a few minutes. Later, one has to try to be known. It's not so easy. In the developed countries the working days are shorter.

The children climb down. The idol opens its eyes and innumerable ribbons come out of its mouth, unwind and float on the air.

POET: What is coming out of its mouths?

CEGESTIUS: Novels, poems, songs.... the machine stops until the next autograph hunters feed it. The rest of the time it digests, it meditates, it sleeps. It has six eyes, and three mouths...and just be sure, don't ask me why.

He leads the Poet off in another direction, to a kind of abyss that they lean over, like Dante and Virgil.

CEGESTIUS: Farewell, this is where I must leave you...I am sorry. Those are my orders.

POET: Who gives them?

CEGESTIUS: Even if I knew, I wouldn't tell you.

POET: Stay with us, Cegestius.

CEGESTIUS: Do you think one can live among men when they have condemned you to death?

POET: Don't leave me. In any case, don't you need a mirror in order to disappear?

CEGESTIUS: Mirrors reflect too much. They reverse images pretentiously and think they are profound.

POET: Do you know any other ways?

Cegestius backs away.

CEGESTIUS: Close your eyes.

He backs further and further away, becomes translucid and disapppears.

CEGESTIUS' VOICE: Open your eyes.

POET: Where are you?

CEGESTIUS' VOICE: Very far, yet very near. On the other side of the coin.

POET: I've said it too often not to understand you.

CEGESTIUS' VOICE: Aren't you tired of wanting to understand everything for the last seventy years?

POET: *(shouting)*
Where are you Cegestius?

CEGESTIUS' VOICE *(in the distance):*
Where you sent me.

POET *(shouting louder, in distress):*
Cegestius!

CEGESTIUS' VOICE *(further and further away):*
Where you sent me.......

The Poet disappears behind some rocks.

The empty washhouse. The Poet goes through it. We hear the invisible washer-women.

COMMENTARY: I was so tired I thought I heard women on their knees, laughing at me, and beating their washing.

The Poet leaves the washhouse, looks at his watch and continues on his road that takes him from one underground vault to another, until he reaches a part of the quarry that looks like an Egyptian temple. Suddenly, he finds himself in

front of a court-usher in a frockcoat, with a chain around his neck, sitting at a table. His right hand, in a white glove, is putting the receiver back on the telephone.

USHER: If you wouldn't mind waiting for a few minutes, the Minister will see you.

The Poet becomes smaller and smaller, in a kind of huge ghostly waiting room.

COMMENTARY: I waited and waited, and waited.

The camera goes several times from the Poet, who is waiting, to the usher.

USHER: In a few minutes, the President will see you.

COMMENTARY: I waited, and still waited!

USHER: If you would be so kind as to consent to wait for a few minutes, the First Secretary of His Most Serene Highness will see you.

COMMENTARY: The minutes were many and still I waited.

USHER: If you would wait a few minutes, His Majesty will deign to see you.

COMMENTARY *(empty waiting room):* If one waits long enough, eventually one turns into a waiting room.

The Poet, visible again, leaves the stone he was sitting on and goes to the usher who is standing behind his table.

USHER: Abandon hope all ye who enter here.

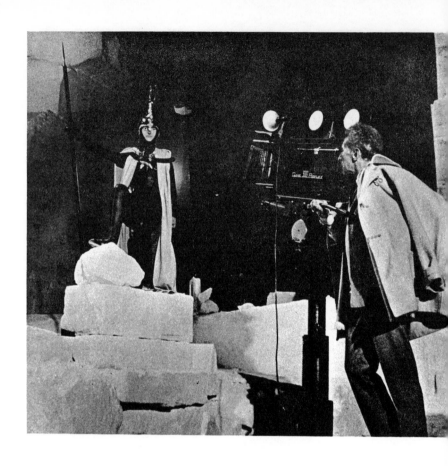

POET: I thought as much. Do I have to write my name on the register anyhow?

USHER (*making a sign with his thumb to the emptiness behind him*):
There's no point in that. Go in without knocking.

The Poet sees the usher and the table melt away. He walks towards a huge arcade.

INHUMAN VOICE OF AN AIR HOSTESS:

> You are requested to fasten your seat belts.
> No smoking please.
> *Vous êtes priés d'attacher vos ceintures et d'éteindre vos cigarettes.*
> *Sie werden getbeten, ihre Gürtel festzuchnallen und nicht zu rauchen.*

The Poet arrives at Minerva's chamber. The Hibiscus re-materializes in his hand. We see what he sees.

In the distance on a kind of monumental stage, is Minerva, flanked by her guards, the man-horses.

Minerva, leaning on her spear, is carrying a shield with a Gorgon's head on it, and a helmet with a swan's neck. She is wearing a black, shiny frogman's suit. The Poet goes towards her and offers her the flower. But she turns away.

POET: Lazarus didn't smell too good either. There is even a painting where Martha and Mary are holding their noses with a cloth . . . I'm sorry . . . I . . . I'm sorry. . . .

As soon as he has walked away, Minerva brandishes her spear and throws it. The Poet is walking. The spear sinks into his back, between his shoulders.

Front view. The spear has transfixed the Poet and come out through his chest. He raises his hands to it, and falls to his knees, then lies on his side, murmuring over and over:

> How horrible . . . how horrible . . . oh, how horrible. . . .

Minerva and her entourage.

The man-horses come down off the stage.

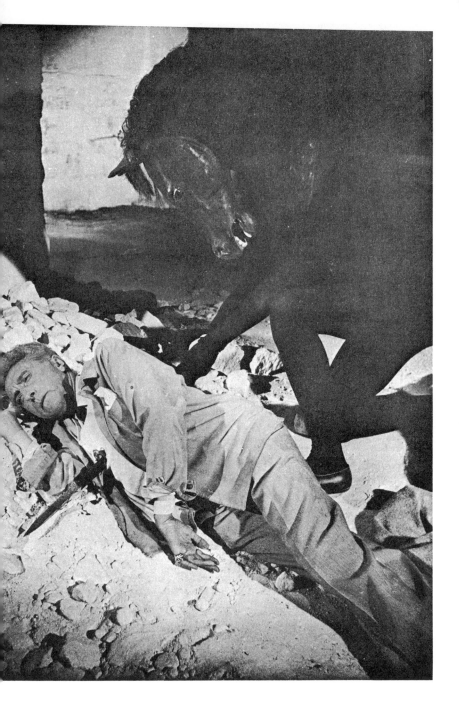

One of them pulls the spear out of the Poet's body.

They lift up his body and carry him away.

The blood that was under his body and the Hibiscus that had fallen on the ground turn red.

Several of his friends are watching him die.

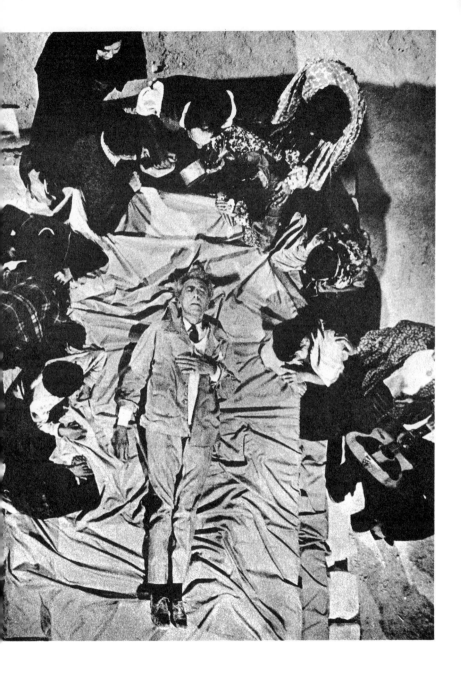

Sitting amid rubble and barbed wire, as though in the Presi-dent's box at a bullfight, are Jacqueline Picasso and Lucia Bosé. Standing behind them are Picasso and Luis-Miguel Dominguin.

Perpendicular view of a tombstone that the man-horses lay me down on.

The gypsies gather round it and mourn. (These scenes are all accompanied by the cymbals and drums of the Seville pro-cession.)

Close-up of the Poet's face, with wide-open false eyes. Smoke curls slowly out of his half-open mouth.

COMMENTARY: Pretend you are crying, my friends, since poets
    only pretend they are dead.

The Poet, without bending his knees, rises upright onto the tombstone.

He leaves the tomb and the gypsies, comes out of the quarry through a huge split in the rocks into the countryside, hesi-tates for a moment as to which road to take, and appears to answer the call of an almost unbearable ringing sound, like the note "A" from a tuning-fork.

The Sphinx.

The Sphinx, the trunk of its body a woman's, gently waves its long white-feathered wings and slides along a wall over the Valley of Hell. The Poet walks past without seeing it, as he still has artificial eyes.

Oedipus.

Oedipus, blind, leaning on Antigone, comes out through one of the gates of Thebes, whispering incomprehensible words. He walks past the Poet who does not see him.

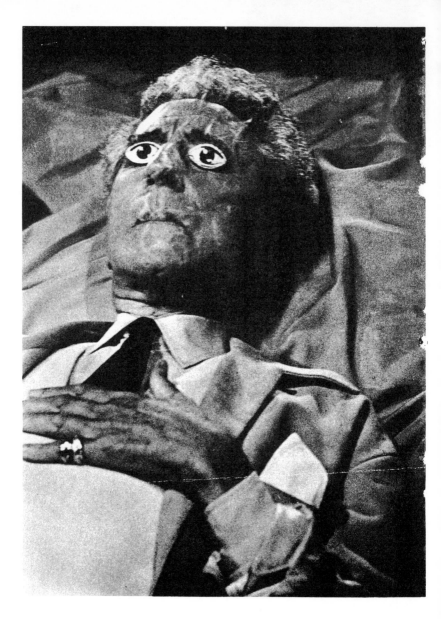

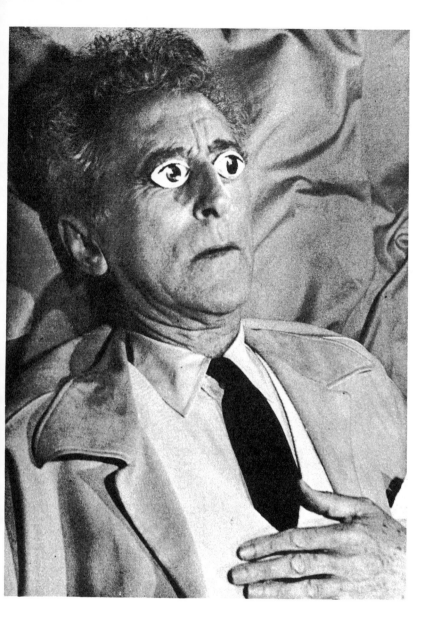

COMMENTARY: The Sphinx, Oedipus ... It is possible that one
day we can meet those we have been too anxious to
know, and not see them.

The Poet, still walking, on another road in the Alps.

COMMENTARY: I awoke from this walking sleep on a road, and
while I was wondering which way to go, I thought I
heard the motor cyclists from my film *Orpheus*. I knew

what they were doing. I would have to undergo the same death as Cegestius.

He stops at a bend in the mountain road.

I was wrong. It was only the police.

The Poet realizes that it is not the black angels from Orpheus *but only the police.*

FIRST POLICEMAN: Your papers.

POET: Why?

FIRST POLICEMAN: I don't have to give you any explanation. A man on foot is automatically suspect.

He goes off to join his colleague.

Cegestius materializes on the face of the rocks, goes up to the Poet and pulls him toward the place where he had appeared.

CEGESTIUS: Quick, quick, follow me.

He seems to be crucifying the Poet on the rocks by the edge of the road.

CEGESTIUS (*shouting in a tempest*):
After all, the earth is not your country.

They disappear together.

The motorcyclists realize who it was and go back to apologize.

SECOND POLICEMAN: We've only got to ask him for his autograph.

FIRST POLICEMAN *(no longer seeing the Poet):*
>   Well, of all the . . . !

The policeman, stunned, drops the Poet's identity card which turns into the Hibiscus flower as it touches the ground.

A sports car full of young people.

They get out at the top of the slope and rush down at top speed in a great tumult of shouts and laughter and jazz.

The policemen mount their motorcycles and give chase to the young people.

The flower flutters in the dust and disappears off the screen.

The car disappears into the distance, followed by the motorcycles, revving and back-firing.

COMMENTARY: And that's all. A joyful wave has swept across my farewell film. If it did not please you, I am sad, for I gave it all I could, as did the least important workman on my team. . . .
>   My star is a Hibiscus flower. You may have recognized several well-known actors along the way. They did not appear because they are well-known, but because they correspond to the roles that they play, and because they are my friends.

My hand finishes the drawing of Orpheus' profile.

The soap bubble turns into smoke and the smoke turns into the words

>   The End.

Films directed by Jean Cocteau (1889-1963)

Le Sang d'un Poète (The Blood of a Poet)	1930-32
La Belle et la Bête (Beauty and the Beast	1946
L'aigle a Deux Têtes (The Eagle Has Two Heads)	1947
Les Parents Terribles (The Storm Within)	1948
Orphée (Orpheus)	1950
La Testament d'Orphée (The Testament of Orpheus)	1959

In addition, Cocteau worked as a scriptwriter on *La Comédie du Bonheur* (1939), *Le Baron Fantôme* (1943), *L'Eternel Retour* (1943), *Les Dames du Bois du Bologne* (1944), *Ruy Blas* (1947), *Noces de Sable* (1949), *Les Enfants Terribles* (1950), *La Princesse de Clèves* (1960) and *Thomas l'Imposteur* (completed after his death in 1965).

A FILM TRILOGY

———

Through a Glass Darkly
The Communicants (Winter Light)
The Silence

———

INGMAR BERGMAN

Translated from the Swedish by Paul Britten Austin

Ingmar Bergman's theme in this great trilogy of films is the obsession with God; that strange, compelling search for guidance which is, perhaps, doomed by the very contingency from which it springs. Bergman calls his treatment a 'reduction':

Through a Glass Darkly — certainty achieved
The Communicants — certainty unmasked
The Silence — God's silence — the negative impression

Ingmar Bergman's ability to combine the greatest universality with the most delicate intimacy of situation and characterization gives his films something of the power of myth. David, the father in *Through a Glass Darkly*, tortured by his daughter's madness and by his own fascination with it; Tomas, in *The Communicants*, the doubting priest who lacks the strength to abandon the corpse of his faith; Anna, in *The Silence*, left with no guidance but the demands of her body and the bitter disapproval of her dying sister — all these are recognizably figures in a modern cosmology of the spirit.

The quality of Ingmar Bergman's writing is such that these scripts are almost as rewarding to read as the films are to watch. The volume is illustrated with stills from the three films.

PERSONA AND SHAME
Ingmar Bergman

Translated by Keith Bradfield

'It was fairly obvious that the cinema should be my chosen means of expression. I made myself understood in a language that by-passed words, which I lacked, music, which I have never mastered, and painting, which left me unmoved. Suddenly, I had the possibility of corresponding with the world around me in a language that is literally spoken from soul to soul, in terms that avoid control by the intellect in a manner almost voluptuous.'

This extract from *The Snakeskin* (which was written for the presentation of the Erasmus Prize in 1965) provides a remarkable key to the two recent filmscripts contained in this volume. *Persona*, which is not technically a script, but rather a frame-work for a movie, totally involves the spectator in the action. He is forced to participate in the erosion of the distinction between the personalities of the two main characters, Elisabeth, an actress who has suffered a complete nervous breakdown and Alma, her apparently well-balanced and extrovert nurse. The relationship turns into a bewildering reversal and substitution of their respective identities.

Shame has, seemingly, a more straightforward and clearly defined plot. In it we watch Jan's progress from artist to survivor/murderer in a war-torn society. The progressive breakdown of all civilised standards of behaviour in his environment have completely brutalized the hero, and his culture and morality are shown to be only superficial attributes, easily annihilated by the massive unconcern of an arbitrary and amoral universe.

FACE TO FACE
A film by
INGMAR BERGMAN
Translated from the Swedish by Alan Blair

Face to Face is Ingmar Bergman's exploration into the mind and emotions of a clinical psychiatrist whose efforts to cope with her life and career drive her to attempt suicide. It is her shockingly quick breakdown and agonizing rebirth that Bergman has tried to describe.

Before starting on this film, Bergman wrote the following letter to the cast and crew: "We're now going to make a film which, in a way, is about an attempted suicide. Actually it deals ('as usual' I was about to say) with Life, Love and Death . . . I think that for some time now I have been living with an anxiety which has had no tangible cause . . . Another person's vicissitudes came to my aid; I found similarities between her experiences and my own, with the difference that her situation was more obvious and more explicit, and much more painful . . . I have benefited greatly by this process, the torment, formerly diffuse, has acquired name and address. In this way it has been deprived of its nimbus and alarm. If this opus can be of similar use to someone else, the effort is not in vain."

Starring Liv Ullmann and Erland Josephson, the film, whose British release coincides with the publication of this book, has won enormous international acclaim. American reviews described the film as ". . . brilliant drama . . . Mr Bergman is more mysterious, more haunting, more contradictory than ever, though the style has never been more precise, clear, level-headed." (*New York Times*); ". . . like a troubling dream until one is forced, in a strange way, to confront one's own doubts and fears." (*Daily News*); "Ullmann has never been better. Hers is an intelligent, devastating performance." (*Time Magazine*); "Magnificent . . . wonderfully reviving in its command and charity." (*The New Yorker*).

Ingmar Bergman has been one of Europe's leading film and theatre directors for thirty years. His most famous films are *The Seventh Seal, Smiles of a Summer Night, Through a Glass Darkly, Persona, Cries and Whispers, Scenes from a Marriage* and *The Magic Flute*. Bergman has received every major American and European film prize and is considered by many to be the world's greatest living film director.

INGMAR BERGMAN
The Cinema as Mistress
Philip Mosley

Ingmar Berman's work is both influential and highly acclaimed, leaving its mark indelibly on a whole generation of cineasts. Many of his films, notably *The Seventh Seal, Wild Strawberries,* and *Cries and Whispers* have been hailed as classics. Bergman has made over 40 films in a period spanning nearly three decades. Many are closely related to each other through Bergman's personal pre-occupations and meditations. All of them bear the mark of his highly individualistic treatment of such universal themes as human isolation, relationships between people, man and his search for God and the position of the artist within society.

Philip Mosley's study is primarily a critical history of Bergman's films dating from his earliest work as a writer/director in the late 'forties right up to *Autumn Sonata* and his first projects outside of his native Sweden. The author traces the development of Bergman's highly individual techniques, dialogues and his dis-jointed use of time and space in the narrative. Mosley sees Bergman's cinematic innovations as a product of his own sense of identity as a Scandinavian artist. He stresses the importance of Bergman's personal biography, especially his early life and experiences in Sweden as the son of a Lutheran Minister.

A useful and provocative companion to Bergman's films, this book includes many stills from Bergman's more famous films.

Formerly a lecturer in Comparative Literature at universities in Australia and the US. Philip Mosley is currently a freelance translator.

'...a solid introduction to the work of the master...' *Times Literary Supplement*
'...excellent study...' *Sunday Independent*

SCENES FROM A MARRIAGE

Ingmar Bergman

Translated by Alan Blair

When Ingmar Bergman's *Scenes from a Marriage* was first serialized (in six parts) on Swedish television, practically the whole country stayed home. Streets were deserted and appointments cancelled while everyone followed the terrible and very moving story that might have been their own. Bergman has taken the most banal of situations, a seemingly perfect marriage that goes wrong, and turned it into a drama that strikes all too close to home.

The television production, of which this book is the script, has now been adapted by Ingmar Bergman into a commercial film which was recently premiered in the United States, and will soon be distributed worldwide. Starring Liv Ullman, Erland Josephson and Bibi Anderson it was described as 'intensely, almost unbearably moving.' The *New York Times* said: 'Mr Bergman is examining the molecular structure of a human relationship. You think you've seen it before, but every time you see it, it's new, which is one of the things about love.'

This work, as much a novel in dialogue as a script, is certainly Bergman's most ambitious, one that clearly follows in the tradition of the 'marriage plays' of Ibsen and Strindberg. It is an intensely personal and truthful drama. As Bergman himself says: 'This opus took three months to write, but rather a long part of my life to experience. I'm not sure that it would have turned out better had it been the other way round, though it would have seemed nicer.'

Ingmar Bergman has been one of Europe's leading film and theatre directors for thirty years. Some of his better known films are *The Seventh Seal, Smiles of a Summer Night, Persona, The Virgin Spring, Through a Glass Darkly, Silence*, and *Cries and Whispers*. He has won virtually every major European and American film prize and is considered by many to be the world's greatest living film director.